dedicated to *Joshua*

D0219377

Salinan Indians
of California
and their neighbors

BETTY WAR BRUSA

NATUREGRAPH

Salinan Indians of California and their neighbors

Library of Congress Cataloging in Publication Data CIP

Brusa, Betty War, 1920–
    The Salinan Indians and their neighbors.

    (American Indian map book series, v. 2)
    Bibliography: p.
    1. Salinan Indians. 2. Indians of North America-California.
I. Title.   II. Series.
E75.A53 vol. 2   [E99.S17] 970.1s   [970.3]   74-13249

1989 Printing.

Copyright © 1975 by Betty War Brusa

ISBN 0-87961-023-9 Cloth Edition
ISBN 0-87961-022-0 Paper Edition

Books for a better world

Naturegraph

DISTRIBUTED BY:
LANGTRY PUBLICATIONS
7838 BURNET AVE.
VAN NUYS, CA 91405-1051
FAX (818) 988-0037

ACKNOWLEDGMENTS

I wish to express my thanks and appreciation to everyone who has helped me gather information for this book. My gratitude and special thanks go to Eugenie Bonnot for independently illustrating this book in the spirit of the Salinan Indian culture. The literature of Ralph and William R. Rambo of Stanford University and that of Raymond Friday Locke have given me invaluable help. Dr. A.L. Kroeber's research in his books was a wonderful guide to follow. I also am grateful for the help of the San Antonio Valley Historical Society, Monterey County Historical Society and Mariposa Historical Society, and for the help and patience of many gracious librarians. They are listed below by name and library:

Cipriano Avila, Jolon area (Deceased)
Mrs. Nita Baughman, Monterey County Library
Mrs. Mary Jo Brazil, Salinas Steinbeck Library
Dolores Encinales, Jolon area (Deceased)
Mrs. Geraldine Horn, Monterey County Library
Mrs. Louva Huntington, Monterey County Childrens Librarian
Mrs. Lois Koolwyck, Librarian for Monterey County
David Mora, Jolon area (Deceased)
Mrs. Margaret Pass, Monterey County Library
Mrs. Mable Powell, Palma High School Librarian
Mrs. Patricia Washmundt, Monterey County Library

I express especial thanks to my husband Adolph for his understanding and assistance throughout my years of researching and writing this book.

TABLE OF CONTENTS

Division I   Salinans

Division II   Neighbors of the Salinans

INTRODUCTION

We are all cognizant of the continual altering of the scene in the Salinas Valley and the extraordinary speed at which the alterations take place. It is interesting therefore to return to the beginning, to the period of perhaps the first resident, the very nearly forgotten Salinan Indian and his neighbors. A major change took place with the arrival of the Spanish explorers, the missionaries, and the first white settlers. The effects were profound, and for the Indian desolating.

The Salinans were one of the happy, contented groups of California natives whom the "advantages of civilization" have swept into oblivion by a continuous series of actions carried out on an extensive scale by the invading white man. The Salinans ultimately succumbed to the successive aggressions of the missionary era and the ensuing Mexican and American periods.

In a land of variety such as California, where unlikeness in language and culture distinguished the smallest divisions of the numerous stocks, it is difficult to separate and state definitely the characteristics of any group. This is especially true in the case of the Salinans. They had no written language and today we derive our sparse knowledge about them from the memories of a few remaining Indians, biased mission records, and uninterested pioneer accounts. Therefore, this writing is an endeavor to reconstruct a picture of at least some of the Salinan culture, from any source which has become available to the author.

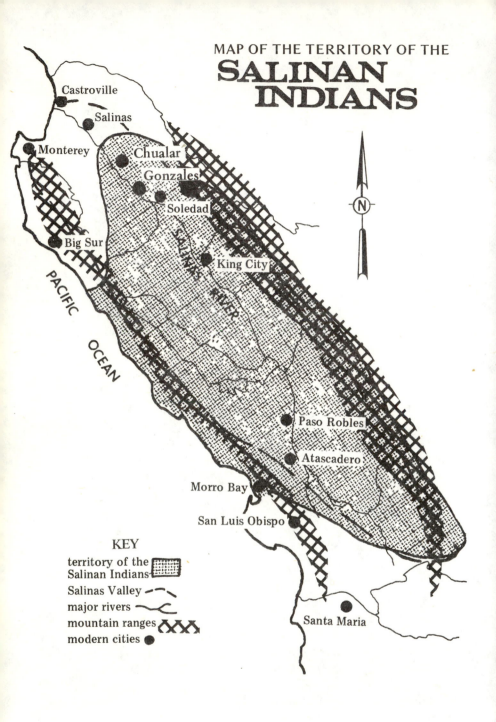

MAP OF THE TERRITORY OF THE
SALINAN INDIANS

Castroville

Salinas

Monterey

Chualar

Gonzales

Soledad

Big Sur

SALINAS RIVER

King City

PACIFIC

OCEAN

Paso Robles

Atascadero

Morro Bay

San Luis Obispo

Santa Maria

N

KEY

territory of the Salinan Indians

Salinas Valley

major rivers

mountain ranges

modern cities

1

LOCATING BOUNDARIES

GEOGRAPHY

The Salinas River winds its way along the floor of the Salinas Valley. It is the third longest river entirely within California and the largest "submerged" river in America. The source of the Salinas is in the mountains a few miles east of San Luis Obispo, and it meets the Pacific Ocean near the small community of Castroville, northwest of Salinas.

The main tributaries of the Salinas are: the San Lorenzo River, which flows southwest from the El Gabilan Mountains on the east wall of the Salinas Valley, emptying into the Salinas near King City; the Estrella River which rises in the mountains dividing the Salinas Valley from rivers draining to the south; the Arroyo Seco River which rises in the Santa Lucia Range, flows northwest and joins the Salinas about one mile south of Soledad; and the San Antonio and Nacimiento Rivers, both of which rise in the Santa Lucias and flow southeast, parallel to one another, for almost thirty-two miles, joining the Salinas north of San Miguel.

The Salinas Valley totals 4,780 square miles and has about 651,000 acres of broad, fertile bottom land. It is 150 miles in length and its maximum width is about 45 miles. It stretches from the high mountain area in southeastern San Luis Obispo County to Monterey Bay, 82 miles south of San Francisco. The Salinas Valley shares alike with other Coast Range valleys a northwest-southeast course. On the east it is separated from the San Joaquin Valley by the Diablo Range and from the San Benito Valley by the El Gabilan Range. The Salinas Valley lies entirely within the boundaries of Monterey and San Luis Obispo Counties.

It is one of the most productive valleys in the United States. The soil varies from decomposed granite to thick, rich adobe, but comprises in larger part the light-weight and heavy-weight sandy loams. Its lower end is definitely a delta area, and deltas usually mean agricultural production. The depth of the soil is great, with the water level near the surface. The great body of bottom land is so fertile that it has been spoken of as "The Valley of the Nile", and is also known as "The Salad Bowl of the Nation".

According to the geologists the changing of the land in the Salinas Valley is a remarkable one. The present view of the mountains and valley is that they are of late occurrence, the minute parts having been carved from sedimentary rocks of the first period of the Cenozoic era. The core of the El Gabilans and Santa Lucias is older, supplying materials for some of the later rocks.

Approximately 175 million years ago (Jurassic period) in place of the Salinas Valley there was a restricted width of granitic elevated ground reaching northwest to what are now the shores of the Pacific Ocean.

To the west, the Pacific Ocean received from the mountains of this ancient "Salina-Land" huge deposits of sediments which were ultimately united as the Franciscan Series, forming the mass of the southern area of the Santa Lucia Range. To the east was a wedge-shaped abyss engulfing northwestern California, originating southeast of Paso Robles.

During the time of the Cretaceous period (65,000 millennia) a great amount of the area was salt marsh (restricted remains of water inundation). Previous mountains had been worn down and were now layers of sediment deposited on the floor of the great abyss that engulfed much of northwestern California west of the Sierra Nevada.

When the Rocky Mountains began to form, toward the end of the Cretaceous period, the land of the salt marsh was so old that it was reduced to a level plain.

The Santa Lucia and El Gabilan Mountains began to form after the Tertiary period, that is in the Pleistocene epoch, perhaps 1,000 millennia ago, and were undoubtedly then much higher than they are today. The great continual erosion carved out the present form of the mountains and deposited much silt in the northern area of Salinas Valley. Drainage from the Salinas and the interior valleys of California all poured into Monterey Bay and dug out deep canyons which today can be followed under the sea, with depths of more than 7,000 feet recorded. After years of slowly decreasing erosional forces the lower section of Salinas Valley was again under water. In the Sierra Nevada during separate intervals low temperatures and heavy rains and snows brought on glaciation. In the Santa Lucia Mountains evidence of glacial activity has never been found; the rugged, carved ridges and deep canyons are undoubtedly the result of severe weather conditions, raging torrents carrying earth and rocks into the valley of the Salinas River.

Then came the period of carving out of the present characteristics of Salinas Valley, and arrival of the Indian.

LANGUAGE

The existence of the Salinan group as an independent linguistic unit was first agreed upon by Major J.W. Powell in 1891, following Dr. H.W. Henshaw's detailed examination of the California Indians in 1884. He took the name, Salinan, from R.G. Latham, who had applied the term to the original residents of the Salinas Valley. Latham used the name on a wider scope than Powell, as he included the Esselen, the Ruslen, the Carmel and the Soledad dialects of the Costanoan family. For many years the similarities of the languages of the southwest California Indians were argued, but since the publication of Powell's "Indian Linguistic Families", the independence of the Salinan, Costanoan, Esselen and Chumash languages, one from another, has not been disputed.

The Salinan language, however, had a remote resemblance with the Esselen, and also had some similarity with the Chumash. These three languages comprised the central California members of the Hokan stock. Other members of this linguistic stock were: the Northern California Chimariko, Karok, Shastan, Yana, Pomo, Washo, and the Yuman of southern California.

Hokan was possibly the most widespread, and perhaps formed the most ancient language stock in California.

TERRITORY

Very little is known concerning the boundaries of the Salinan territory. According to A. L. Kroeber their territory stretched from the headwaters of the Salinas River, or possibly from the area of the Santa Margarita divide, north to the Santa Lucia Peak and to an unknown area somewhere south of Soledad. It is possible also that the boundary was somewhat north of San Luis Obispo, probably at San Miguel. It may be assumed for present purposes that Santa Lucia Peak was the northern limit of the Salinan, since it was reported to J. Alden Mason that the mountain was shared equally by the Soledad (Costanoan), and the Antoniano (Salinan). This peak, the tallest in the region, could serve as a natural division point, and the statement is therefore plausible. From the Santa Lucia Peak the boundary would run generally north and east to the boundary of the Yokuts, and southwest to the coast in the area of Lucia. The exact boundary between the Salinan and the Yokuts, according to Taylor, was not known. It has been an accepted theory that the

Salinan eastern boundary extended to the top of the Coast Range, the watershed between the coast and Tulare Lake. While this belief is supported mostly by negative proof, it is believed that the Yokuts did not reside west of the range.

The town of Cholame was at the foot of the Coast Range, though the Salinan village Cholame is said to have been the closest village to the San Miguel Mission. The lands of the Coast Range were undoubtedly hunting grounds and probably had no large, permanent villages.

There is nothing recorded concerning the boundary of the Salinan and Esselen groups.

DISTRICTS

The country is extremely rough. The Santa Lucia Mountains rise abruptly from the shores of the Pacific Ocean and form the west wall of the Salinas Valley. On the Pacific side they are in many places without plains or even what might be called foothills, and some of the hundreds of peaks are over 5,000 feet in elevation. Along the valley side of the Santa Lucias are foothills covered with sagebrush and oak trees.

Inland from ten to fifteen miles it is extremely mountainous and almost impassable. The area is thickly wooded and trenched with deep canyons, the streams small and unnavigable. The Nacimiento and San Antonio Rivers have cut narrow gullies running southeast.

Oak trees of several species are abundant, and redwood trees grow in the mountainous area near the ocean. Bears, deer, antelope, mountain lions, wild sheep, coyote, ground squirrels, skunks and rabbits are common. The only poisonous animals are rattlesnakes and scorpions. Many species of birds are found, including mountain quail, California quail, swallows, mourning doves and the horned lark. Of freshwater fish the trout is the most representative.

DIALECTS

The Salinan language comprised three dialects. Along the rugged, harborless coast, Playaño (Of-the-Beach People), was spoken. The mountain and valley areas were divided between the northern Antoniano and southern Migueleño dialects. Records have been preserved for both dialects. They were named after the San Antonio and San Miguel missions.

Dr. Henshaw recorded that he was informed each village had a different dialect.

SETTLEMENTS AND PLACE NAMES

According to A.L. Kroeber, there were twenty Salinan villages known other than as "just names"; some are placed on the map (in front of book) with question marks. Location of Lema, Ehmal, Tsilakaka and Ma'tihl'she are undetermined other than being mentioned as on the coast. Troloe was located at points so greatly separated as Santa Margarita and Cholame. Cholame, the important village of the San Miguel division, is proclaimed by some to have been located at the San Miguel Mission, others state it was on Cholame Creek. With the Cholame Land Grant lying along this creek, and the Spaniards' being quite definite in their applying native names, the latter locality seems right. However, it was the custom of the Salinan Indians to name streams after areas at their mouths. The lower course of Cholame Creek flows into the Salinas River near the mission (this lower course is now called Estrella Creek). In this way the name Cholame may have been, rightly enough, taken up stream by the Spaniards. The opinion lacks sufficient proof, but is all that is known on the disputed points. The majority of Salinan villages seem to be located on the Nacimiento and San Antonio Rivers. In part this irregularity results from lack of interest of the missionaries in preserving native knowledge. Even in the dry, unfruitful hills of the Cholame drainage there were probably as many villages as in the valley proper.

18 The Salinan Indians

A. S. Taylor copied the names of many of the Salinan villages, from mission records, and was successful in locating some.

Atnel
Chacomex
Chitama   in the mountains near the coast
Cholueyte
Chunapatama   (see Chitama)
Chuquilin   San Miguelita
Chuzach   on Monterey River
Ejmal   on the beach
Ginace
Iolon   on Rancho los Ojitos
Lamaca   on the shore
Lima
Quina or Quinada
Seama
Steloglamo
Subazama

PRE-MISSION HISTORY

The scarcity of our knowledge of the Salinans results in part from lack of interest of the white man, at what may be called a conciliatory time, before the Salinan culture was reduced. Indications are that the time before Europeans came was tranquil; the Indians of the territory seem to have been a contented people and showed little interest in warfare.

First to behold the Salinan territory was Juan Rodriquez Cabrillo, who, in 1542, sailed up the coast to Cape Mendocino. He saw no Indians and reported the coast to be uninhabited. In 1602, sixty years later, Don Sebastiano Vizcaino skirted the coast on his way to Monterey Bay. A few rush canoes put out to meet him from a bay said by A.S. Taylor to be, "probably San Luis Roadstead or that of San Simeon".

If it were the former port, the natives were probably Chumash, while if from the latter port they may have been Playaño (Salinan).

The true discoverers of the group were the members of the Gaspar de Portola expedition of 1769. During about three weeks they encountered seven villages of inhabitants. Portola estimated their particular numbers at, 60, 30, 80, 400, 60, 200 and 220. Not all were on his direct route of travel. As Chumash, Esselen or Costanoan villages were included, the figures shed little light on the numbers of the Salinan family; they are, however, of interest in supplying an average of over 100 people per village.

2

ECONOMIC LIFE

FOOD

There were many species of acorns, many seeds and fruits, one red in color and round like a cherry (madrone), three varieties of sage (chia), one a bulky type like a lentil, the other two slimmer. While it is not definite, it is possible that the acorns from the live oaks were used for mush, those of the deciduous oaks for making bread. Of the live oaks three species were used; the white oak followed in the order of preference.

The acorns were stored in granaries until ready for use. Tall basket-like containers, made from the slender branches of white willow, were constructed on the ground adjoining the house, without bottom or stone foundation. They were lined and covered with grass.

Acorns were gathered, stored, dried, cracked, ground, leached and usually cooked with hot stones in a basket. When being ground the meal was kept from scattering by the use of a flared, hopper basket.

The gruel made from the gathered acorns was known as acorn mush or soup; usually the mush was thicker, less watery than the soup.

When ready for use the desired amount of acorns was removed from the granary, carefully broken open with a small stone and sun-dried. When thoroughly dried the seeds were pounded, or ground, in a stone mortar until they became a fine meal. After the meal was ground it was leached in a basket, the stitches of which were adequately spaced to allow water to percolate through.

During the cooking process the hot stones had to be stirred to make certain heating was done evenly and to prevent holes being burned through the basket. The mush or soup was nourishing, rich in starch, and when prepared from some species of acorns perceptibly oily. Acorn bread was baked in earth-ovens. Cakes of meal dough about three inches in diameter were placed between two layers of damp grass and cooked all night.

Seeds of many plants were consumed and undoubtedly served an important role in the Salinans' diet. The seeds were harvested with seed-beaters and baskets, then stored in seed-granaries until ready for use. When ground they were boiled in the cooking-baskets to make soup or mush. The seeds were not parched on trays with hot coals, the usual California custom. The staple seed, wild oats, covered the rolling hills in many areas. The seeds of three varieties of grass were consumed, also the seeds of sage, chia, and wild sunflower.

In common with other California Indians the Salinans were referred to as "Diggers", in the early days. The origin of the title has been traced to the first immigrant whites who observed Indians digging the roots of plants with a digging stick. The plant, *Yucca Whipplei*, widespread in the Santa Lucia Mountains, was subjected to virtually the identical treatment wherever it grew. The roots were dug with a stick and then cooked in an earth-oven for two days. The fruit of the *Yucca Whipplei* was either eaten raw or baked in the earth-oven also. Another use of the Yucca plant was for soap. After washing, the large roots were pounded on a boulder; the roots were then rubbed over their bodies and into their scalps.

Clover, of which three varieties were distinguished, was a delicacy and eaten raw with no preparation. Buckeyes were consumed, but only after the poison they possess was leached out, as was the custom among the Yokuts and other neighboring tribes. Wild blackberries, strawberries, elderberries, gooseberries, toyon berries, choke cherries, camass (Indian potatoes), prickly-pear cactus and numerous other fruits and berries were eaten.

Because of the Indian's use of the pine (*Pinus Sabiniana*) of the mountains as a source of the pine nuts, the early settlers called the trees Digger Pines. The name has become recognized and accepted for that species of pine tree. Mushrooms probably were not eaten by the Salinans, but were a favorite food of the Monterey Costanoans and the Yokuts.

The Salinans were virtually omnivorous. Of the larger game, bear, particularly the grizzly bear, was not often eaten. This was possibly due to their ferocity as well as to the shamanistic supernatural power and human resemblance attributed to them. Among the smaller animals, dog, coyote and wolf seemed to be taboo. Of the birds, hawks, condors, owls, buzzards and eagles were not consumed, due to the Salinan's feeling of deep respect for them. Many reptilians and some insects were avoided. The Salinans' diet resembled the Miwoks' much more than that of the Yokuts, for the Yokuts ate skunk and tabooed the carnivorous birds.

Such snakes as were eaten were cooked in the hot ashes of the fire. The Antonianos, the more northern group of the Salinans, were reported to have relished lizards, but they were not eaten by the Migueleño. Larvae of the yellow-jackets were placed individually on a spit and held over the fire, then eaten, or were ground and stirred into the acorn meal mush.

Seafood undoubtedly supplied a principal part of the nourishment of the people residing on the coast. Those inland possibly caught suckers and trout in the smaller streams, and speared salmon in the Salinas River. Some proclaim that journeys were made to Tulare Lake for fish. Bullheads and an unidentified fish, were taken in the ocean, as were clams, red and blue abalones, and unidentified shellfish, possibly mussels. They were eaten either raw or cooked. Crabs were favored as well as seaweed. The latter was stuck on a stick to be heated over the fire and eaten with bread or mush, possibly for its salt flavor.

All meat was prepared in one of three ways. If needed for immediate use it was roasted over open flames or in the coals of the fire. For gradual use it was baked over night in the earth oven, and would keep a week or more. If it were necessary to keep the meat a longer time it was sun and air dried, or "jerked". Meat was rarely if ever boiled in the cooking basket.

The cooking basket in which the boiling was done was watertight and was used all over California. The food to be cooked was placed in the basket and covered with cold water. Heated stones were continuously added until the water was hot enough to cook the food. The earth-oven was also very nearly a universal method of cooking and was made by digging a hole in the earth which was lined with stones and a fire built on them. When the stones were heated the fire was removed, damp grass laid over the stones, and the food to be cooked placed in the hole and covered with more damp grass or leaves. Small sticks and dirt and more heated stones were laid over the hole and left for a desired length of time. The heat was retained and the food cooked slowly. Most foods cooked over night, while others required a longer period of time, sometimes two days.

Fire was made by twirling a drill of poison-oak wood upon a hearth of dry willow twigs. Two men, to relieve one another and thus continue the friction, were often needed for this procedure.

HUNTING AND FISHING

The Salinan groups fell into two divisions, having linguistic, cultural and physical differences, that is the fishing people on the ocean, and the hunting people in the mountains. The coastal group undoubtedly hunted and the inland people possibly made journeys to the coast to obtain seafood. Although the area of the San Antonio Mission is not more than eighteen miles from the ocean, the ruggedness of the intervening mountains made of this relatively short distance a difficult journey. It is doubtful therefore that the trip was often made by the inland villagers, or vice versa.

Game was plentiful in the Santa Lucia Mountains, and provided the group with animal food.

Deer were generally hunted by stalking, a method used among all Indians. The Salinan hunter covered his head with a stuffed deer head and his body with the attached hide. A deer, or antelope, was skinned with great care, leaving the horns attached to the hide. The well preserved head was stuffed with dry grass to maintain the shape. The hunter wore the shell like a cap. When sighting the prey the hunter would cautiously drag himself slowly along the ground using his left hand for balance. The right hand carried the bow and arrows. The direction of the wind was determined by dropping a small amount of loose dirt, and the deer was approached from the "leeward" side. A good hunter imitated the movements of the deer so perfectly that he could get close enough and kill several of the animals before others in the group suspected danger. The bow was held horizontally, not perpendicularly, when hunting large game, as the Salinan believed the arrow thus carried more power. Men hunted in small groups or individually. The shaman supervised prayers and a pipe smoking ceremony while the hunters talked to their bows and arrows, asking them to fly straight and swift. Prayers offered by the shaman were for "deer power" for the hunter. The cautious hunter chewed tobacco constantly as he approached the animal, "believing this tended to make it drunk and less wary".

Bears were caught by placing a trap near the animals' accustomed trails or caves, or bait was put out and the men hid in holes or behind rocks near by, from which the bear could be shot several times with no danger. Among the Migueleño division, according to Mason, small game, such as rabbits and small birds were caught by the use of nets. Snakes were caught by the use of sticks.

The use of fish hooks and lines is not a matter of record among the Salinan. It is possible that the Playaño people had developed fishing methods of their own for the procuring of seafood, but as they have long since disappeared any knowledge of their culture has vanished with them.

ARCHITECTURE

The houses of the Salinans were possibly of several types. The common house was quadrangular in shape but made without excavation, and was about ten feet in diameter. A post was erected at each corner and one in the center. Four roof poles connected the center and corner posts and across these other poles were laid. The roof was covered with a thatch of bundles of rye or tule grass lashed on with strips of withes or bark. The walls were made of tule. A smoke hole was left near the center of the roof and the fire built near the middle of the hut; the entrance being merely an opening in the tule.

Sweat houses were usually small, hemispherical, partly subterranean structures. A circular excavation approximately four feet wide and a foot in depth was dug and brush placed around, arching over to meet at the top. Deer skins were spread over the brush, and mud was heaped on to keep them in place and to retain heat. The fire was built in the center of the floor and the bath taken in the smoke and heat.

DRESS AND PERSONAL ADORNMENT

Generally speaking, the Salinan men wore nothing in the summer. Upon occasion women wore an apron, usually consisting of two pieces, front and back. In winter both sexes wore robes, or blankets, of woven rabbit fur or tule grass, and a coating of mud might be smeared on the body to help resist the cold. Moccasins were unknown. Basket hats were worn by the women and possibly by the men when carrying burdens.

The Salinans wore their hair long and the men's beard was

plucked close. No red-shafted flicker headbands, feather robes or aprons or other feather ornaments were remembered by a few surviving natives in 1884. The use of feathers for decorations by the San Joaquin Valley Yokuts is known. The only reference to feather ornaments was that to feathers attached to the shaman's stick, with single eagle feathers extending from the forehead forward: these were used by dancers during the "Kuksui" dance.

Nose ornaments were not used but ear ornaments of abalone shells were worn.

Face or body tattooing among the Salinans is unknown.

They did paint themselves on frequent occasions. Red, white, blue and yellow seem to have been their favorite colors. The red was made from cinnabar, and yellow from the root of a plant, possibly *Psoralea macrostachya.* The blue might have been "wad" (bog-manganese) used by the Chumash. The source of white is not known.

TRANSPORTATION

The Salinans generally abiding in one place were possibly given little to travel. Their territory was restricted and quite mountainous, with the rivers unnavigable. The occasional trek to Tulare Lake and possibly to the ocean for fish accounted for most of their migrations. It is doubtful that the inland people made rafts or boats. The Playaño, or beach people, must have constructed some type of boat or raft, possibly made of driftwood.

Burdens of all description were probably carried on the back. A large burden, or carrying, basket was conveyed from one place to another by means of a cord of bark which went over the forehead and was attached to the burden basket.

Babies were carried in the universal cradle. This was of a triangular shape, the framework composed of two strong sticks laid across to form a back. The baby was strapped on by strips of rawhide, with a band going over its forehead.

As little or no snow falls in the Salinans' territory the use of snowshoes was unknown.

MONEY

Beads established the criterion of wealth. Salinan manufactured beads were of abalone or mussel shell, in three colors. The blue beads were of the greatest value, pink beads prized for their shininess were second, and least were the white beads. The blue beads were elongated and the shells were taken from an unknown locality, some distance away. Two of these made a man independently wealthy according to Alden Mason's records from the missionary. These may have been the money of the northernly peoples, as suggested by Dr. Henshaw.

MEASURES

The Antoniano Salinans determined the time by the moon, the new moon being the point of departure. Time of day was decided by the position of the sun. Night was irregularly divided into intervals, as darkness, midnight and on until dawn.

Other measures were primarily for length, but may be used also for beads. Small objects were measured by the distance between the tip of the thumb and the tip of the little finger when the hand is fully extended. This was called "tolma'n", "one hand", by the Antoniano, "ma'wu" by the Migueleño. A lesser measure was used by the Antoniano, the width of the thumb. "Tewai' yutopoka", an Antoniano term, was an arm's length measured from the tip of the thumb and forefinger joined. The span of the outstretched arms was used by both Antoniano and Migueleño; it was measured across the breast. Placing the tip of the thumb against the forefinger, was a term meaning "two—". A pace, or step, was used in measuring short distances.

Long journeys were approximated by suns. Seeds and other commodities exchanged in trade were measured in baskets of standard size. The names of four sizes of baskets were: "spo'kaiha", "kilpa'hl" "wukkupt", and "s'la".

MANUFACTURES

With the exception of basketry, the subject of Salinan manufactures would be pertinent more to the topic of archaeology than to that of ethnology. Few articles of any description of Salinan manufacture are in existence, and except for some articles of wood all of them are stone implements of which it can be stated only that they were discovered in the area of the Salinan group.

BASKETRY

The Salinan baskets that have been preserved are very few,

and are probably all of 1884 manufacture. The University of California possesses thirteen of the baskets, constituting probably the majority of the Salinan baskets in existence. No baskets of any great age are known; neither has any description of Salinan basketry been recorded. It is evident that under such conditions no challengeable statements concerning Salinan basketry can be made. The knowledge and art of the baskets in existence must be accepted as typical of the group.

Little is known concerning the native basketry of the Salinan, Costanoan and Chumash, but it is assumed that they followed the typical technique of coiled weaving. Twined weave was used for most ordinary purposes for which coiled weave was unsuitable.

The granaries, for storage of acorns and seeds, previously mentioned may be termed basketry. They were constructed of white willow twigs interlaced. They were approximately two feet in height, three feet across at the bottom and sloping inward, leaving an opening of about twenty inches, making a container of a truncated-cone shape.

Large burden baskets, about thirty inches high, were also constructed of white willow, the exact shape unknown.

The seed-beater, was a looped stick of oak. They did not make basketry beaters, but shallow, coiled trays were used for that purpose and for winnowing seeds.

Basketry hats were of a coiled weave; the exact shape is unknown.

The customary coiled baskets and trays were made in various sizes and shapes and adapted to sundry uses. The ordinary deep baskets were used for cooking, storing, and for keeping water in the house. Trays and bowls up to twenty inches in diameter were used for many purposes. Baskets with fine intervening spaces were used for leaching acorn meal.

Small trinket baskets, were made of twined tule grass in various sizes and shapes for different household uses.

A group of grass stems tied together, usually about seven or

eight, formed the foundation for the coil of the Salinan basket. The sewing was done in splints of "bunch grass". The grass was kept in water until ready for use, when it was taken in the fingers and teeth and split in half. The splints were scraped to a uniform size, width and thickness, and sewed around the coil with the aid of a bone awl, each stitch including several of the stems of the coil below and usually appearing below two of the stitches of the coil below, the latter rarely divided. They averaged between fifteen and twenty to the inch and the coil foundation was rarely seen. Borders were finished in a plain coil, the end being inconspicuous.

A different type of coil was that of a tray. The foundation was of a large, coarse grass, the woven piece a broad, thick splint, with the stitches far apart, four or five to the inch. The border was finished in a double-strand braid.

In the coiled baskets the coil runs in a clockwise direction. Coiled baskets with grass foundation were held with the inside to the weaver, the coil proceeding clockwise in that position, and the sewing was introduced from the inside.

The only native decorative material was black from the root of the fern, *Pteridium aquilinum.* The fern root was kept in water until desired, and was sewn in place of the weft material when it was desired to have a design.

The materials used for weaving twined basketry were limited to two, white willow and tule. The white willow was used for large and coarse work only, such as the granaries and twined carrying baskets. Tule was used for the small trinket baskets. These were of various shapes with variations in the weave.

Both woof and warp of twined weave were of the same material, young shoots of tule and twigs of white willow, with the weaving done in double-strand twining. Tule baskets were started with four thick bundles of young, dry shoots with the bundles arranged in pairs, one pair over and at right angles to the other pair. Around these bundles two strands of tule grass were twisted, the bundles gradually separating into smaller numbers and finally into single warp parts as the thickness of the basket increased, and the weft parts enclosed progressively fewer

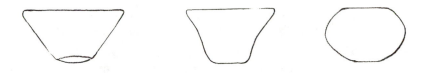

warps at each twisted strand. Additional warp materials were added as needed, the ends were allowed to stick up about an inch on the outside until the basket was completed, when they were cut off close to the basket. As new weft cords were needed, the preceding cord was laid parallel to a warp cord and included in the twine, which required no cutting of the end. The end of the new weft was left sticking out like a new warp element until it was cut off. The majority of the baskets were made with a constricted top, the width of the opening being smaller than the widest part of the basket. To accomplish this the width was lessened by pulling the warps closer together, by combining several warp elements in one twist of the weft.

The border was completed in one of two ways. The warp materials may have been turned over outward and caught under the last row of twine against the next warp to the left. The more common finish was a double border. The warp materials, after being caught under the last row of twine, instead of being trimmed off were intertwined to form an outer border. Passing down through the last row of twine they passed under the end of the second warp to the right, turned upward and to a height of about one-eighth of an inch above the inside border, over the end of the next warp to the right and turned down under the second warp to the left and were trimmed off.

Decorations in tule baskets were made by changes in the weave, mainly by crossing adjacent materials, the twining starting a short distance above when the materials had again separated to their normal distance. The twine is continuous, passing over the crossed warps at a slight angle, at which point a double crossing of the warps was necessary due to the double width. Some irregularities of weaving ofttimes occurred, possibly due to the requirements of the weave.

STONE WORK

Many mortars and pestles of various sizes and shapes have been recovered throughout the Salinan territory. Some are of irregular shape, others have a rounded exterior, and some are of a truncated-cone shape.

Mortar holes in bedrock are still being discovered throughout the area. The holes are of various depths and sizes.

Making mortars by attaching basket-hoppers to unworked boulders was possibly the method used by the Salinans. Portable mortars were used upon occasion, without the basket-hopper attachment.

Tiny mortars are also found in the area. They vary from six to eighteen centimeters in diameter, and are made of sandstone of various degrees of hardness. The grinding hole is usually smaller in proportion to the magnitude of the mortar than is the case with the larger mortars. They were probably used for powdering pigment such as red ocher.

Pestles and mullers were probably used for the same purpose. They varied from twenty to twenty-five centimeters in length. Some were irregular in shape. Mullers were used as pestles, being differentiated from the latter mainly by a shorter length and by flattening of one side.

The pestle was held near its upper end. As it was raised the wrist was turned until the stone was half horizontal; on the stroke it was twisted back and fell perpendicular. The wrist movement probably saved raising the pestle to its full height. The woman laid her legs over the rim of the mortar to hold it steady and thereby brought herself closer to her grinding.

OTHER MATERIALS

Baked clay pottery among the Salinan is unknown.

No great activity in feather working has ever been recorded, and the best known of bone objects seems to be the simple awl. It was made by sharpening the end of the ankle-bone of a deer. Mats of tule are unknown.

A carrying net was made of deer skin. The skin was cut into strips and the net made by tying the strips together at the corners by the use of milkweed twine.

3

SOCIAL LIFE

PUBERTY

Ceremonies accompanying adolescence were of great importance throughout California. The ceremonies for the two sexes differed.

The girl was secluded in a small hut set apart from the village for four to seven days and nights. The taboos she was expected to observe were numerous. She was not to look at the moon or sun, she could not touch her hair, and she ate from her own special baskets. At the completion of the seclusion period she was allowed to bathe. According to their belief the girl was now a purified woman. A feast was held in her honor and the food was furnished by her family for the entire village. There were several taboos observed by the women during the menstrual period. They ate and slept in seclusion, cooking and eating nothing greasy. At the end of their seclusion they were purified by bathing in the river.

The influence of the toloache, or Jimson weed (*Datura meteloides*, a large white bell-like-flower plant), extended to the Salinans from southern California. A brew with a narcotic effect was administered to the young men so that they might see clearly and be able to detect witchcraft. A dance was held and the young men threw sticks at a ring of wood. The most successful player was awarded a charm to make him an excellent hunter and a wealthy man.

MARRIAGE

The Salinan marriage custom required only that the suitor

request the bride from her parents, and upon occasion it sufficed that the chosen girl consented to the marriage. When a young man and woman appeared together, both marked by fingernail scratches, (symbols of love and matrimonial benevolence) they were known to have contracted marriage on the preceding night.

There were restraints (taboos) between young married couples and their parents-in-law; any communication between them was avoided, except in cases of emergency.

BIRTH

When a woman was about to bear her child, she was taken to a brush hut, by a fresh-water spring, accompanied by another female. The hut contained a short, shallow trench heated with small, hot rocks. This was covered with a frame of willow and woven tule grass covered with pine needles. The woman lay on the warm bed during labor. When the baby was born the umbilical cord was cut with a sharp stone and the cord tied with a strand of split tule grass. The baby was immediately bathed in the spring. Two days later the new mother was about her daily work, but she remained in seclusion for a month. She was not allowed to bathe, eat greasy foods or walk any great distance. The baby's umbilical cord was observed closely, and when it fell off a special feast was celebrated. A few restrictions had to be observed by the father too. He took care not to do such things as smoke his pipe, become angry, or to commit any other acts considered indiscreet by the society.

Soon after birth the baby was strapped into a cradle. In the winter months a rabbit skin was tucked in around the child. Dry grass pounded until soft was used for diapers. The basket cradle was carried on the mother's back; wide deer-sinew straps attached to the cradle were worn across the mother's chest and forehead. The baby was tied in the cradle with lacings of deer sinew, in a sitting position with its feet dangling.

The child was usually four to six years old before it was given a name. The shaman possibly bestowed the name and the entire village celebrated the "baptismal". The meanings of recorded Salinan names are unknown, but it is believed the children were sometimes named for trees.

Children were wanted and if a woman was unable to produce she was considered a social outcast and her husband usually divorced her.

The education of the children consisted of what their parents taught them. For example the fathers taught their sons how to use the bow and arrow. The boys practiced their lessons in the fields, hunting squirrels, rabbits, mice and other small animals. The women took their girls with them so that they learned to gather seeds, and accustomed them to carrying the burden basket.

SICKNESS

A serious or prolonged illness was considered as having a personal cause, earthly or supernatural. It frequently was thought to be caused by evil magic and was counteracted by the services of the shaman. Minor problems of physical health were often treated without the shaman, either by the use of herbs or by a medicine formula. In the case of herbs, many of the natural pharmaceutical properties of Indian remedies are recognized today. They were believed to possess sympathetic magical powers sufficient in themselves to counteract the magic of the disorders.

Bleeding, scarification, sweat-baths and the use of herbs comprised the curative practices of the Salinan. There was no singing or dancing around the patient as among the Yokuts.

White willow was considered to be an excellent cure for a fever. Twigs were boiled in water and the liquid was given to the patient to drink. Curative herbs were generally chewed by the shaman and/or some other person and spread on a wound. Red ants were allowed to bite the part of the body swollen and affected. Their use may have been due to the belief in fighting fire with fire, a performance ofttimes used among peoples of today.

In the event of serious diseases and broken bones toloache might have been used as an opiate. Tobacco played an important part medically. It was eaten or chewed. A native species of *Nicotiana* was used, the leaves crushed and steeped in water and the mixture drunk. Intoxication and nausea ensued, usually followed by a deep sleep and a healthy appetite the next morning. It was considered excellent for stomach pains.

DEATH

Among the Antoniano the most distinguished dead were cremated, while those less noteworthy were buried. Among the Migueleño all are said to have been buried.

On the death of an Antoniano native all of his personal belongings, including his house, were immediately burned, and the village was abandoned for a short time. If cremated, the ashes were gathered and scattered toward the west. The deceased's name was never spoken, as it was considered a serious offense and all of his relatives endeavored to forget him. No ceremony accompanied the burning or the burial and no annual tribal mourning ceremony was ever recorded. There were some few who set out food on the graves so that the soul would have enough to eat when returning to the island in the "big waters" to be reborn.

The dead of the Migueleño stock were wrapped in skins and a ceremonial burning of personal possessions was held. The bow and arrows of the deceased were put on a high pole in the center of the village and around this inhabitants gathered, the relatives on one side and the other people on the other side. The relatives brought out all of the personal property of the deceased and piled it at the bottom of the pole. As each article was tossed down it was the right of any villager to seize any item he desired and attempt to escape with it. If he could evade the pursuit of the relatives and run the course around the village three times, it was his right to retain the item. If caught, the item was returned to the pile with the other possessions and burned. When the usual ten days of mourning ended the house of the deceased was burned and a new one was constructed and occupied by the family. After a "reasonable" length of time it was customary for the widow's relatives to find her another husband.

A ceremony of mourning was held by the people about one year later.

The family of the deceased had their hair cut as a sign of mourning, but nothing is known concerning other mourning customs.

TERMS OF FAMILY RELATIONSHIP

A list of terms of relationship for each dialect was collected by

Dr. Henshaw in 1884, other lists were secured by J. Alden Mason, and an effort was made to fit them into a definite system. The designations will be discussed under particular categories.

Two terms for father and two for mother existed in each dialect, Antoniano, father Tele', ekc; mother, Apai', epx; Migueleño, father ta ta', pexk; mother apa 'i, e'pex. A few of the Antoniano terms are listed:

My father	tele [ekc]
Your father	tuM'e'kc [tum-tele']
His father	e'kc - o [te-tele'-o]

My mother	apai' [e'pax]
Your mother	t!me'epax [tum-apai]
His mother	e p'x-o [apai-o]

The Migueleño stock made no distinction for the sex of children, i.e. the term pase'L was used for both. The sexes were distinguished by the Antoniano: "as" son, and "te'co", daughter. The same distinction was observed in the Antoniano word "stexa" for boy and "stua", girl, opposite to the Migueleño's "a p'xa", child. The word "as" son, might have been used only by the men, as the term "ti'co" seemed to be the women's word for both son and daughter.

Following are the terms for grandparents and grandchildren: though there is a resemblance in both dialects, there are variations in meaning.

	Father's Parents	Mother's Parents
Antoniano	xala'	nene'
Migueleño	ama'	nenE'

The term "xala' " has been said of both dialects as meaning "grandfather" of either parentage. The term "nene" or "nenE" was used by both dialects and sexes equally and possibly indicated maternal grandparents.

The reference to grandchildren shows a reciprocity with the grandparents.

	Son's Children	Daughter's Children
Antoniano	ta'iyaL	tciya'
Migueleño	tema'k	tena'iyaL

Ta'iyaL was given as grandson, at times as grandchildren; Tcaiya', when used meant granddaughter. Tema'k is the plain reciprocal of ama', meaning son's child. It was possibly exclusively a woman's term. Greatgrandchildren, "mace'l", great-great-grandchildren, "setilka'i".

Distinguishing characteristics for comparative age and sex are made and reciprocal relations noted.

	Elder Brother	Elder Sister
Antoniano	kai	pe'
Migueleño	kaiyE'	pepe'

	Younger Brother	Younger Sister
Antoniano	tos	t'oN
Migueleño	tos	t'oN

Uncle and Aunt would be expected to be words from those combined for father and mother. It has been noted that such was not the case.

	Father's Elder Brother	Father's Elder Sister
Antoniano		pas
Migueleño	La'pac	

	Father's Younger Brother	Father's Younger Sister
Antoniano	ta'	
Migueleño	Ek!a'	apa'c

The reciprocal nephew and niece resemblances are clear. Possibly no more than four terms in either dialect occurred here. There is no record of more.

	Child of Elder Brother	Child of Elder Sister
Antoniano	tak	
Migueleño	tE'nak	

	Child of Younger Brother	Child of Younger Sister
Antoniano	tE'paeek	e'axa
Migueleño		tEmasa'XE

The oldest uncle is said to have been called "sak" by his nephews among the Antoniano and the children of the oldest brother were termed "tA".

Names For Relatives By Marriage

	Husband	Wife
Antoniano	la	se
Migueleño	laN	seN

	Son-in-law	Daughter-in-law	Older Brother's Wife
Antoniano	te'leM	tuke'wi	tim ta'L
Migueleño	te'leM	tE'mai'	

Independent of dialect differences, there are approximately thirty-four terms recorded pertaining to actual family relationships. Organization of the family and such other affairs as might be considered under the present subject have little additional information which could be passed on. See appendix for other Salinan dialect terms once used.

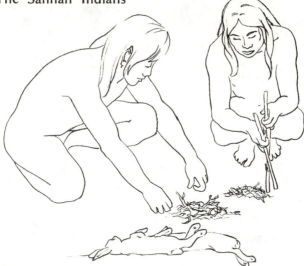

GOVERNMENT

The village chief was chosen for his bravery by the elder males of the village (according to J. Alden Mason). Besides the Salinan's village chief, there were district chiefs who commanded three or four villages, with the village chiefs as subordinates. Each chief in his village collected a personal offering each day, which might consist of game, fish, fruits and seeds. Everything that the village chief collected daily of the villagers he sent to the district chief, who every ten to fifteen days visited his district, and each village received him with ceremony. They presented the district chief with gifts of the most valuable things they possessed, and appointed a few young men to accompany him to the place where he resided.

The chief did not hunt or fish—it was done for him by the male members of his family. The chief walked around the village each morning and evening speaking to everyone and family arguments were ofttimes settled by him. It was also his responsibility to declare special days of rest, after all work was completed.

If anyone committed a theft, the accuser appealed to the chief, who gathered a legislative body and deliberated with them as to the punishment and the amends that were to be made. If the theft was a useful article, or something to eat, the punishment for the penalty of theft amounted to returning the stolen article or its equal, but if a maiden was stolen, the abductor was compelled to marry her. The same punishment was handed down in a case of rape, even when not accompanied by abduction. The village chief was required to report upon any incident whatever, to the district chief, sending to him any law breaker, with the charges against him. During the trial the accused, man or woman, stood with the hair hanging loose and covering the face.

The importance and power of the chief seemed to be greater among the Antoniano Salinan, Obispeno Chumash, and certain Costanoan groups than usual, and the general social organization, especially among the Salinan, followed in many ways that of the Yokuts. Whether or not the Chumash allowed their chiefs the privilege of polygamy among their other privileges is unknown.

DANCES

Virtually every occasion of social gathering in the California Indian villages was accompanied by some diversity of dance, a custom which appears to have been particularly well developed in the western portion of North America. Dancing furnished a great part of the shaman's mysterious powers, assisted him in making use of and conquering magic, in preventing death, and in conversing with the spirits. It also supplied a great amount of social enjoyment for the people. Disastrously, all native dances of religious consequence were strictly forbidden by the missionaries and as the result many of the dances and their origins disappeared.

Many of the Salinan dances were carried out by individuals, while spectators supplied the musical accompaniment and singing. The music was created by cocoon rattles or split sticks, rasps, whistles or rattlesnake rattles. Cocoon rattles are reported to have been used exclusively by singers at a dance. Rattlesnake rattles were used by the participants. The flute and possibly other musical instruments were played at dances.

The Kuksu'i dance seems to have been the most popular among the Salinans. Two dancers impersonated the god or spirit Kuksui and his consort. The singers sat in a row singing and clapping their hands; no rattles or other musical instruments were used. In front of the singers the two dancers executed the dance naked and painted red, white and yellow. A headdress of feathers was worn, reaching to the shoulders, and with eagle feathers extending from the forehead forward.

Animal dances were performed, the Coyote, Bear, Owl and Deer dances. These were executed by individuals, the dancer imitating the action and the cry of the animal. Each dance had its own song, with only two now known. The Bear dance was performed in August when the outlook for an abundant crop of acorns was good.

hau'-wa-ya	he'-ne-ye
hau'-wa-ya	he'-ne-ye
	he'-ne-ye
hau'-wa-ya	he'-ne-ye

["There's plenty,   we are glad"]

     ta-we' — ye-he'
     ta-we' — ye-he'

["We're chewing acorns"]

     hu' — hu' — hu'

The Owl dance was a favorite of the Migueleños, in April

     pa' — na-ta   pa' — na-ta   co'ko — nai
     pa' — na-ta   pa' — na-ta   co'ko — nai

["Dance,   dance,   owl."]

     tro' — ki-kup' — ic — tun   tro' — ki — kup' — ic — tun
     tro' — ki — kup' — ic — tun   tro' — ki — kup' — ic — tun

["In the   cave,   In the   cave"]

     hu — hu — hu'
     hu — hu — hu'

Group dancing was enjoyed upon very special occasions. The dance among the Salinans was performed by a row of men and a row of women, alternately, dancing and resting. The women's portion was termed "lole'i". Approximately ten singers, with rattles, accompanied the dancers.

When there was a new moon the shaman danced while the older men sang:

> "The moon is born and soon will
> die to be born again so that we
> who are born and die will be born
> again."

GAMES

Amusement of several types was enjoyed by the California natives, helped by the fact that villages were permanent; acorns and game were very plentiful and easily accessible; and wars were at a minimum. A great portion of the amusement was made up of games of skill, strength and endurance, but games of chance were also prominent.

The popular game, "peu", common to practically all of western America, was frequently played by the Salinan. The objects were either three shells joined or an eagle's bone, one being unadorned, the second with a fibre string tied around the middle of it. The players formed two "sides" but the actual playing was limited to two men on either side. Only one pair of bones was used, each of the players hiding one bone, while the opposing side attempted to guess the hiding place of the unmarked bone. Both men on the inactive team guessed at each occasion and paid for wrong guesses with counters. Ten to fifteen counters were used and much betting was done by both sides. If both players were incorrect with their guesses two counters were paid to the opposite team; if one guesser was correct, one counter was paid. The teams alternated in hiding the bones. When a man was unlucky he gave his place to another member of his team. Women sometimes took their husband's place in the game while he rested. The game was played by the Costanoans, according to A.L. Kroeber, in practically the same manner.

The women played a game, "tecoinE'", with ten bones which were thrown with a basket. It was probably the common dice game played by women over much of Western America, using walnut-kernels, acorns or split and burned sticks. The relative number of reverse and obverse sides showing decided the count. It was the most common and popular gambling game for women. The hoop-and-pole game was played at the young men's puberty ceremonies. According to Henshaw, a game, "me'nakwa'kwa", was played by two persons who locked their middle fingers and pulled to see which one was the stronger.

When the wet or cold weather forced the Indians to remain inside the family played a game with a hidden piece of bone which was passed from hand to hand under rabbit robes. One person guessed who held the bone. The popular game of today, "button, button who has the button", undoubtedly derived from the Indians' "family game".

TRADE

There was a great deal of interchange between the Salinans and the Yokuts and commodities were undoubtedly exchanged. Journeys were made frequently by each group to the territory of the other and a friendly understanding evidently existed. The manufactured shell beads of the Salinan, which could not be obtained by the Yokuts other than by trade, and other unknown products were bartered. The amount of trade with Chumash, Esselen and Costanoan is not known, but was possibly very limited. From all that has been reported and recorded, there were strict boundary lines between the Salinan, Chumash and Costanoan. The Indians learned these boundaries when they were small children. Considerable hostility existed between the language groups.

WARFARE

California warfare seldom reached any great consequence, and its part in the native plan of life was very trifling when compared with the warfare of the Plains and Eastern woodland Indians. The lack of tribal unity in California except possibly among the few southeastern stocks, prevented the development of war-like tendencies. Among the Salinans so-called wars were hostilities of a few days' duration, and were usually settled quickly with the shedding of very little blood. It has been said that as mountaineers, the Salinans were probably more warlike than the valley and coastal peoples surrounding them, but proof of this belief is lacking.

4

AESTHETIC PURSUITS

MUSIC

Several types of rattles were used. The split-stick rattle was the most common. The stick was split, and bound with grass twine at one end to prevent it from separating. When used, the thumb was held at the binding and the rattle struck sharply on a tree or rock. Rattles were also made from the rattles of a rattlesnake, and from cocoons. The cocoon rattles were used by the Salinan singers at a dance. They were made by tying several cocoons to a stick. A musical rasp was used, a notched stick rhythmically rubbed with another. Whistles may have been made from reeds. A flute, about five palms long, was played. Eight tones were produced perfectly. Various tunes were played; most of the tunes were gay and all in one measure.

The Mission records reported: "In singing they raise and lower the voices to seconds, thirds, fourths, fifths and octaves. They never sing in parts, except that when many sing together some go an octave higher than the rest. Of their songs most are merry, but some are somewhat melancholy in parts. In all these songs they do not make any statement (proposition) but only use fluent words, naming birds, places of their country and so on."

In reference to some singing an octave higher the statement probably means some sang in a falsetto voice.

RELIGION

The care of the dead and the belief in disembodied spirits of the deceased which prevails not only all through California but through-out practically the entire world is significant of a universal belief in immortality. The belief in the power of the shaman, or medicine man, was possibly more strongly developed among the Salinans than was usual in California.

The strong influence of religion in their lives was such that it must have entered into practically every phase of life, aesthetic, social, economic or mythological.

Religious Conceptions

For facts on the religious life of the Salinan the principal source must be taken from the records of the early observers, and they, unfortunately, were very biased in their point of view, and observed the native customs with prejudiced eyes. A.S. Taylor wrote, "The Indians of the San Antonio believed in a Superior Being; they believed he made the sun, moon, stars, earth, men and all visible things." This is a doubtful report. Fages, claimed that idolatry was greater among the Salinans than among the Chumash, due to the plurality of gods which they adored. Father Francisco Palou on the other hand declared that idolatry did not exist.

The belief in a previous as well as a future life seems to have been part of the Salinan religious creed.

Shamanism

The shaman, among all the tribes of California Indians, owed his importance to the personal, magical relationship which he had with supernatural beings, objects and forces. The power was attained in various ways among different groups of Indians. The Salinan method was probably in obtaining the amulet, or charm. A person decided as a young boy that he wanted to be a shaman, and would learn secrets of magic from an old shaman and practice that magic. By trading his dreams and visions with the practicing shaman he learned more secrets. In California, medicine women usually possessed far less potent magic, and were unknown with the Salinan. The shaman's stick with powerful magical possessions was used by him in his incantations, with other material objects and charms. His pipe was similar to the ones used by the villagers, but was decorated with paint. Possibly the majority of his possessions were differentiated from those of ordinary persons.

MYTHOLOGY

Early Salinan Legend

In 1773 a Salinan Indian woman (believed to be a centenarian) related to the San Antonio Mission padres that her grandfather told her stories about a man who visited their land upon four different occasions—each time arriving on the wings of a large bird. His clothes and teachings were identical to those of the mission San Antonio padres.

At one time a Spanish nun proclaimed that she and others possessed miraculous powers. They claimed to have been carried on the wings of their guardian angels to pagan countries where they preached the "Holy Word". The story was handed down from generation to generation and the Salinans might have confused the story of the nun with the padre. Some of them believed that it was the padre who had arrived on the wings of the bird.

The story of the seventeenth century padre still remains a mystery, with what may be the only visible evidence of his visits on the walls of the "Painted Caves", five miles above the San Antonio Mission. On the walls of the cave are pictographs representing gods revered by the Salinans: water, moon, sun, coyote and others. Among these red, black and white drawings are crude crosses, possibly influenced by Christianity. There is a large cross on the inner wall, to the right of the wide entrance of the cave, and two smaller crosses on the back wall.

According to the book, *The Mission of San Antonio de Padua*, by Frances Rand Smith, the dimensions of the Painted Caves are: height at entrance, 16½ feet; entrance width, 21 feet; extreme inner width, 45 feet; inner depth, 15 to 20 feet. Back from the entrance is a natural elevation forming a shelf—extending across the entire width of the cave at an elevation of about 3 feet.

CREATION MYTH

The myth of the actual creation of the world from earth by various animals points to the south central Californians as the source of Salinan myths. The trinity of creators, however, was not the hummingbird, eagle and coyote as believed at Monterey, but eagle, kingfisher and coyote. The hummingbird seems to have been included by the Costanoan, but other characters were more familiar to the Salinan, Yokuts and Miwok. The successful diving for the earth was done by the kingfisher, not the duck, turtle or mud-hen as among other groups. The eagle, as was general in the area, was exalted in rank, the coyote being a more auxiliary character such as a messenger and helper. However the important parts of both translations of creation are concerned not so much with the actual creation of the world, but with the creation of man and woman and their discovery of their sexual relations. This conception was found elsewhere too, appearing in the creation myths of the Yauelmani Yokuts and the Rumsien Costanoans. The idea of the creation of humans from sticks and bones and their division into different linguistic groups was also a general myth in the area.

In the few myths collected, explanations are recorded for the existence of various languages, death in childbirth, properties of mescal, of the phenomena at sunset, a rock of an odd shape, the black breast of the woodpecker and the gray eyes of the raven.

The Beginning of the World
[Collected by Dr. H.W. Henshaw, 1884]

After the deluge the eagle wished to get some earth. First duck dove into the water but failed to bring up any earth. Then the eagle put a heavy weight on the back of the kingfisher and he dove into the water for the earth and succeeded in reaching the bottom. The sea was so deep that when he came to the surface he was dead. Between his claws the eagle found some earth and after reviving the kingfisher he took the dirt and made the world. Then he revived all the other animals who had been drowned in the deluge, the coyote next after the kingfisher. When the coyote found himself alive again he shouted out for joy and ran around reviving the rest of the animals that he found dead, sending them back to the eagle.

The Creation of Men and Women

When the world was completed, there were as yet no people, but the eagle was the chief of the animals. He saw that the world was incomplete and decided to make some people. From some of the earth brought up by the kingfisher he modeled the figure of a man and laid him on the ground. In the beginning he was very small but grew rapidly until he reached normal size. But as yet he had no life; he was still asleep. Then the eagle stood and admired his work. "It is impossible," said he, "that he should be left alone; he must have a mate." So he pulled out a feather and laid it beside the sleeping man. Then he left them and went off a short distance, for he knew that a woman was being formed from the feather. But the man was still asleep and did not know what was happening. When the eagle decided that the woman was about completed, he returned, awoke the man by flapping his wings over him and flew away.

The man opened his eyes and stared at the woman. "What does this mean?" he asked. "I thought I was alone!" Then the eagle returned and said with a smile, "I see you have a mate!" Then he sent the newly-made couple out into the world, but they did not seem to thrive very well, so at last he sent coyote to bring them to him again. When they came before him, eagle said, "What have you been doing?" "Merely living" was the reply. "What have you been thinking about?" "Oh nothing, just living." So eagle told coyote to go back with them and consider some way by which they could have more company. "Well," said coyote to the man, "you had better make some more men." "How?" asked the latter. "Why with the woman," replied coyote, "that is what she is for." Then he told them to lie down together. "Well, why don't you commence?" "I do not know how." replied man. "Why, lie down close together!" But they did not succeed in finding a way. So coyote went back to the eagle and reported the failure, and was sent back again with further instructions. "The eagle is very angry," he reported, "and he says you must increase." Then he told them the way that eagle said men were to be made. After several mistakes the couple at last found the proper method, and the coyote ran and reported to eagle that all was going well.

Coyote was then sent to find more people. "If you can't find anything but bones," said eagle, "bring them." Many bones were lying around and these the coyote brought back to eagle, who made a man out of each. Each of these bone-men had a different language of his own, and that is why we have so many different tribes and languages.

Then eagle sent coyote back again to the original couple to inquire about them. "I feel a little heavy," said woman. Then coyote told her that she had another human within her and that under certain circumstances she might die bringing it forth. That is why women sometimes die in childbirth.

There were also those Salinans who believed the eagle shaped man of clay, then placed a feather beside him as he slept. When the eagle flapped his wings over the two, man and woman awoke.

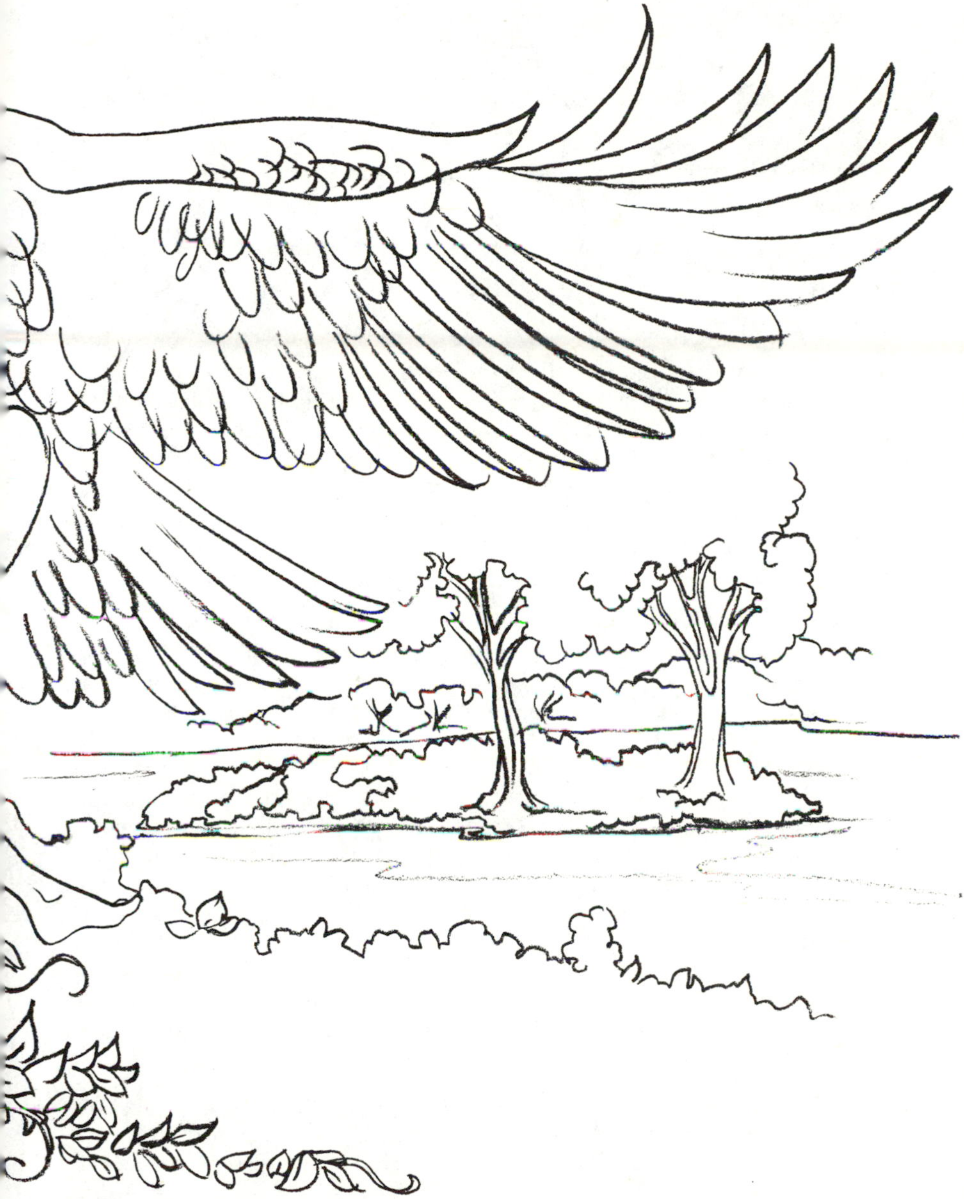

The Deluge

The Salinan Indians had a superstition or tradition of a deluge of water which covered the land in olden times, and believed their priest to be a sorcerer. One of their superstitions was that a hummingbird was first brother to the coyote who was first brother to the eagle.

[The Ethnology of the Salinan; Alden Mason - collected by: Dr. H.W. Henshaw, 1884.]

The Destruction of The Evil Monsters

Many years ago, when all animals were men, the country was full of monsters who preyed on the people. Finally the hawk, realizing the gravity of the situation, persuaded the raven to help him rid the country of the monsters. They set out against a great rock called, "xu'i". Xu'i had a habit of catching people and killing them by throwing them back over his head where a large flock of small birds would feed on the bodies. From their customs of thriving on fat, the birds turned completely black, and were termed, "ka'tca tsani'L". The crow acted as a sentinel for xu'i.

The hawk and the raven came peacefully up to xu'i and the raven, as a brave deed, rubbed his eyes against the rock. They have been gray ever since. Then the two went a short distance off on a hill. "Now is the time!" said the hawk. "I am ready," answered the raven. "But you had best go first!" So the hawk approached xu'i who easily threw him over his head, but the hawk carried with him a small flute and when he stood on it, he always dismounted gently on the ground. Then hawk signaled to the raven and said, "Come along!" The raven was also easily thrown over by xu'i, but as he carried his small guitar with him, he fell lightly on that without any injuries. "Well we have escaped this time," said the hawk. "That's so," replied the raven. "This time I will take the first shot." And he threw a stone at xu'i which left a dent in his head. Then the hawk took a turn and knocked the rock's head off. They then chased away all the small black birds. Xu'i with his head missing can still be seen not many miles above the San Antonio Mission.

Hawk and raven then went to search for another monster, and sought out a terrible two-headed snake. When they approached, the snake, taliyE'KA tapelta, was sound asleep. "Now is the time! He is asleep!" said the hawk to the raven. They made arrows from some reeds growing there and shot at the snake. First the hawk hit him on one side and then the raven hit the other. "Let's go before he gets up!" the hawk exclaimed, and they flew away. They traveled swiftly in the direction of Morro Rock on the sea coast, a well known landmark on the shores of Estero-Morro Bay mentioned by early navigators, but the snake came swiftly after them, breaking down all the trees in his path. "Come on! Don't be afraid!" the hawk who was in the lead kept calling to the raven. Now the dust was close behind, but the hawk said, "When we reach the Morro we'll be safe. The wind will help us there!" At last they reached the Morro, but in spite of the wind's effort to foil him by breaking off pieces of the rock, the snake encircled the rock and began to rise up. "Now is the time! We're going to die! Watch him come!" shouted the hawk. "What are we to do?" asked the raven. "Don't ask me that, just get ready!" replied the hawk, as he pulled a knife and began to hack away at the snake. Then the raven did the same on the other side of the rock, and the snake began to fall in pieces. When he was entirely dead, they went to destroy more of the man-killing monsters.

"Here's another one, and he has a very powerful weapon," said the hawk. They had found the skunk in his hole, but when he heard the noise he came out and turned his tail to them. "Now is the time," whispered the hawk. "Now be ready," said the raven, "I'm going to try first." And he threw a stone at the skunk. The latter turned his tail and fired. Hawk and raven got their flute and guitar while a crowd of people came up behind. Suddenly the skunk made a great smoke. "Look out! Get away before the smoke reaches you!" At last they managed to kill the skunk and went in search of new victims.

"There is one more," said the hawk, "a dreadful one-footed cannibal." The monster was sound asleep when they arrived at his home. "There he is! I'll try first," said the raven. "If I do not kill him you take a turn." The one-footed cannibal woke up and sang a song when he saw the hawk and raven. "Let's shake hands," said he. So the friends went up, seized his hands both together and threw him into a pool of tar. Then they held a consultation as to the best means of disposing of him. Finally they adopted the hawk's suggestion to set fire to the tar. They put some fire on the ends of their arrows and hit him on both shoulders at once. "What are you doing boys?" he cried. "You are treating me as if you weren't my relatives!" Then he started to run, and at every place where the burning tar dropped the mescal began to sprout.

Thus was the land rid of the wicked monsters and enriched by the useful mescal.

Mythological Notes
[Collected by Dr. Henshaw, 1884]

Before the deluge, two mussels lived in a lake, and every once in awhile they caused the waters to rise until a man was thrown in. Finally the male Indians became so few in number that they refused to throw any more men in. Then the mussels caused the waters of the lake and the ocean to unite and the deluge ensued.

Tibe'kenni'c lives where the sun sets. All the dead, good or bad, go there. He swam to the west to escape the deluge, and there he will remain until the end of the world, when he will return. He alone knows when the sea will again rise and overwhelm the world once more. At sunset the dead with Tibe'kenni'c toss the sun up in play. That is what causes the rays of the sun to shoot up in undulations. The red sky is caused by great fires which the people there light to play with.

The eagle was the originator of all things. It was he who gave fire to the Indians.

The skunk was a wizard. His weapon was his urine and with that he was able to kill any living being.

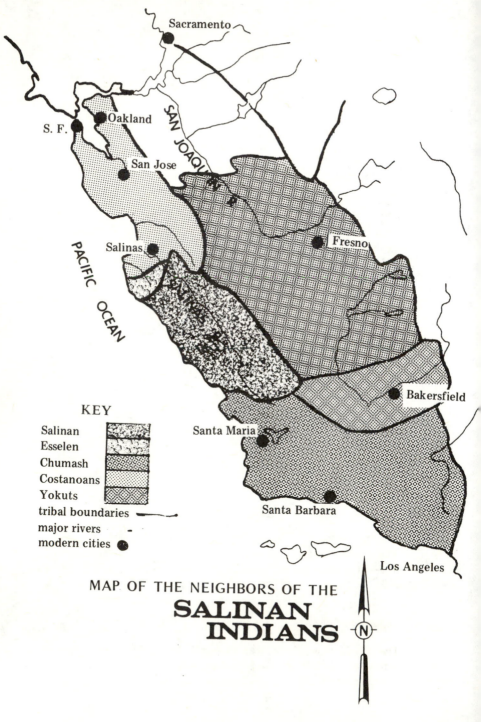

KEY

Salinan
Esselen
Chumash
Costanoans
Yokuts
tribal boundaries
major rivers
modern cities ●

MAP OF THE NEIGHBORS OF THE
SALINAN INDIANS

5

THE ESSELEN

The Esselen were among the least populous of California Indians. Their number has been estimated at from 500 to 1,000, the count of 500 probably being the more accurate. They were restricted in territory and are believed to have been the first group to become extinct after the arrival of the white man.

TERRITORY

Their territory comprised the upper watershed of the Carmel River excluding the lower section where the Costanoans resided, the Big Sur River, and about 25 miles of coast from near Point Sur to Point Lopez. They met their neighbors, the Salinans, at Santa Lucia Peak. To the north of the Esselen lived the Costanoans, on the east and south the Salinans, and the ocean met them on the west.

LANGUAGE

The Esselen language probably is in the Hokan group, though it is not like either Salinan or Chumash, both of which also are of the Hokan family.

SWEAT LODGE

The temescal was a circular ditch dug in the earth and was covered with dirt in a "bell-shaped" erection, leaving a narrow entrance about the size of an oven door. On one side of the ditch the Esselen piled wood and lit it. The men entered the "oven", as many as would fit, and they sang or amused themselves with games.

RELIGION

There is very little information concerning the Esselen religious ideas. They believed that the sun could assume human form in order to kill them, and that after death they were all turned into birds, coyotes and owls, and they revered them all.

MARITAL VIEWS

No Esselen man was allowed to marry more than one wife at the same time. During the time of divorce the husband forced the wife to move out. If he turned her over to another man, that man was obligated to pay the former husband to cover his expenses of obtaining a new mate.

CRIME

Theft was a crime almost unknown. Homicide was punishable by death.

6

THE CHUMASH

The Chumash were at one time considered very important, yet there is little really known concerning them. The Chumash knew the Salinan Indians as, "At'ap-alkulul".

TERRITORY

The Chumash Indians were predominantly coastal people. They lived on the three northern large islands of the Santa Barbara Islands as well as the mainland. It seems that Anacapa was not permanently inhabited. They were thickly populated along the shore from Malibu Canyon, westward to Point Concepcion, and extended northward as far as Estero Bay. Inland they reached to the mountains that divided the direct ocean drainage from the great valley. In the west they lived between the Salinas and the Santa Maria, and short coast streams in the Santa Lucia Range.

LANGUAGE

Only a speculative classification of the Chumash language is possible. That spoken in the San Luis Obispo area, the most northwesterly, between the ocean and the Salinans, was the most divergent. That spoken on the islands was the next in specialization.

CHIEF

The Chumash chief, Wocha or Wot, had influence and enjoyed great honor among his people; he alone had more than one wife. He was summoned to attend all ceremonies, entertain any visitors and his refusal to do so was a cause for war.

BURIAL

The Chumash differed from their neighbors by burying their dead. There was no cremation. Skeletons were as abundant in the Chumash territory as they were scarce in adjoining areas. When prepared for burial the body was tied in a bent position. One man dug the grave and carried the corpse. This custom could indicate their belief in defilement. The members of the village that assisted with the funeral services were paid with shell money. A widow was not allowed to eat certain foods for one year and she wore her dead husband's hair on her head. The burial sites all seem to have been inside of the village and were marked with rows of planks and stones. Tall boards with crude pictures were erected over the prominent men's graves. The mourners danced while singing around the cemetery.

DWELLINGS

Houses were up to 50 feet or more in diameter. The structure was hemispherical, constructed by planting long willow poles in a circle, and bending and tying them together at the top. Other sticks were stretched across the poles, and to them was tied a thick layer of tule mats; sometimes they were thatched. Dirt was not used for protection, except for a few feet above the ground. The frame was too light-weight to support a coating of earth. It is believed that three to four families occupied one dwelling, from 30 to 50 individuals. They were one of the California Indian groups that had what could be termed "rooms", in their houses, and they slept in beds. The beds were crude platforms, raised from the dirt floor. The mattress was a woven rush mat, and a rolled up woven mat served as a pillow. Longer mats were hung around the beds for warmth and possibly privacy.

HUNTING TOOLS

An implement probably rare among the Chumash, and seemingly not known among other California Indians, was the spear thrower. It was a short thick board, almost as broad as it was long, with a groove and point for the butt of the spear. The spear head was of bone, with a barb and chert point. A line was attached to the head, bound on with a cord and a gummy substance smeared over it. The implement was used as a harpoon for killing seals or small sea lions.

The bow used by the Chumash is unknown. It seems they used an arrow made out of cane.

BASKETMAKING AND DISHES

The rushes used for basket weaving were apt to be split with each stitch, the awl passing through or between the hollow and soft stems. Sumac was coiled about the rush (*Juncus* spp.) foundation. The predominant surface, however, at least in decorative baskets, was of rush. Buff, red and yellow undyed rushes were used by the Chumash women in decorating their baskets and water holders.

Dishes and bowls of wood were inlaid with abalone shell. Pots, or "ollas", were vessels made of steatite or soapstone carved into open dishes and almost globe-shaped bowls. Some were up to 2 feet in diameter and thin walled, some were inlaid with small shells. The Chumash also used the boulder mortar, the metate, and a pounding slab with a basketry hopper.

PIPES

Their pipes were a stone bowl, slightly convex in profile, and markedly thinned from bowl to the mouth end. A short bone mouthpiece, was used, set into the stone.

RELIGION

Plummet-shaped charm stones were made much of and considered magic. The native religious customs of the Chumash shaman are unknown. Religiously oriented paintings of great beauty and of many peculiar shapes and designs have been found in caves in the Santa Barbara Mountains.

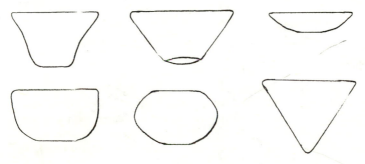

THE COSTANOANS: PENUTIAN SPEAKING PEOPLES

The Costanoans lived in an area that extended from San Francisco and Carquinez south to Soledad, and possibly from the ocean east to the Mt. Diablo Range. Their numbers were estimated at about 7,000.

LANGUAGE

The derivation of their name is from the Spanish Costaños, "coast people". Its awkwardness is to some extent amended by its consistency of use in the literature on Penutian speaking peoples. The name would have been hard to replace by one from a native source, since the words for "men" or "people", varied from dialect to dialect within the stock. Some of the Costanoan divisions were, Mutsun [San Juan Bautista], Runsien or Rumsen [Monterey], and Tamien [Santa Clara]. In the far north, toward San Pablo and Suisun Bays, there was possibly another distinctive dialect, the Saklan, after one of their chief settlements. The extreme southern and northern idioms, Soledad and Saklan, are the least known and seem to have been very specialized. Information on the Costanoan language is pitifully lacking.

VILLAGE NAMES AND LOCATIONS

A series of village names has been recorded but in most cases there is no record of the location of these villages, or of their interrelations as permanent towns. Such villages as have been identified are vaguely located. The ending N, that occurs in many Costanoan settlement names, possibly means, "people of". So does mak, kam or kma, which is plural for "persons". Tak, tka, ta, te is the locative case: "place of". The meaning of me and mo, is similar. Ruk, "house", is used as an ending in the plural sense of "town". "Ocean-at-house", is kalin-ta-ruk, "Chicken-hawk place-houses", kakon-ta-ruk.

FOOD

Among the most important foods for the Costanoans besides acorns were mollusks. Sea lions were hunted, but the manner of hunting them is unknown. There was no way for them to hunt the whale, but when one was washed ashore, food was plentiful. Great kitchen middens or mounds found on the coast and bays contain quantities of seashells.

BODY DECORATION

Both men and women painted and tattooed their bodies. The face tattooing of the women ran in rows or lines of dots.

CHIEF

Unlike their Salinan and Esselen neighbors, the chieftainship of the Costanoan was passed from father to son and his influence and authority are reported to have been limited. Some records state the chief led his men in war.

MARRIAGE

The southern Costonoans practiced monogamy except for their chief. In the north, customs were different. A man usually married his dead wife's sister.

RELIGION AND SHAMAN

The Costanoans did not, it seems, use the Jimson weed. The plant grew in only a few isolated areas in their territory.

Detailed information about religion is sadly lacking. Sun-dances were held and the redwood trees were possibly revered. Offerings were made of acorns, meal, sardines and small pieces of meat on feathered rods.

Any knowledge regarding the shaman is all too vague. When treating a patient it is known he used hollowed bones placed over the affected part of his patient's body to suck out the problem and pain.

MYTHOLOGY

The Costanoans revered the coyote, eagle and hummingbird. One item of mythology was as follows:

Coyote lived in a lonely place. He stood alone waiting for his chief, Eagle, to join him. Eagle rose from a large feather floating on the river. When the water receded that land was explored and people were made, at the direction of Eagle, but by Coyote. Coyote married the first woman, and he and Hummingbird began to have trouble. Hummingbird was so small and swift that he eluded Coyote and even surpassed him. Coyote was very clever, very desirous of all women. He often lost his wife and experienced heartaches. Sometimes he was successful at his schemes to trick humans or other animals or to seduce women or girls; at other times he was defeated or was punished severely.

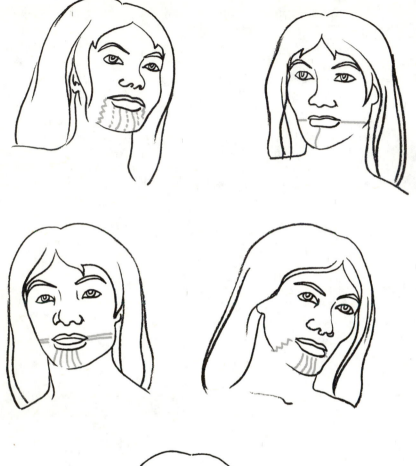

THE YOKUTS: PENUTIAN SPEAKING PEOPLES

The Yokuts tribe occupied almost all of the floor of the San Joaquin Valley, and were found in portions of the foothills as well. Their territory covered between 12,000 and 13,000 square miles, with a population estimation of some 18,000. The San Joaquin Valley Indians had a habitat with sparser vegetation than that of the central and northern California Indians.

LANGUAGE

The Yokuts nationality comprised some 50 tribelets, of which 40 have been located and named. Each of these tribes spoke a different dialect, but the dialects of the adjacent tribes were similar, and comprehensible to each other. Their place of abode was open and communication was not difficult.

GROUP VILLAGES

Members of a Yokuts tribelet lived most of the year in one principal village, having the same name as the community itself. There were also many subsidiary tribelets, one being the largest and considered dominant.

INDIVIDUAL HOUSES

The Yokuts constructed at least five types of houses. The

tribes known as the Hometwoli, Tulami, Chunut, Wowol, and possibly the Tachi, resided in a mat-covered gabled Kawi or communal house. Perhaps each family built its own section. The houses were ofttimes large enough to house about 10 to 15 families. Each family had its own front and back doors in the steep-roofed dwelling, and the doors were covered at night with tule mats. A shaded porch extended along the front of the entire house. Tule stalks were sewn together with an eyed bone needle and strands of split tule grass. The Yauelmani of the southern plains off the lake came near to copying this long dwelling in aligning their wedge-shaped dumlus or tule house, but they kept each continuous family residence separate. The middle plains tribes, the Tachi and Wechihit, built small tule dwellings of a different type, oblong with rounded vertical ends. A ridgepole may have been used on two posts, with five poles planted along each side and bent over the ridgepole. There would have been a door at one side of the first post. The total length of the dwelling was about 12 feet. The covering was of loose tule mats, each stalk wrapped to the next one by a hitch of a single strand of tule grass. Bedding and floor mats were sewn through. The Wechihit used a covering of mohya stems that reached from the ground to the ridge, and were held in place outside by many horizontal stalks tied to the framework. This was called a chi or te. The Yaudanchi, a hill tribe, constructed their winter dwellings of tule, te, of which a variety, shuyo, grows along the banks of the streams to the limit of the plains. It was a cone-shaped house with a hoop at the top to attach and separate the leaning poles of the framework, leaving a smoke hole. The dwellings were built in rows.

When camping in the hills during the summer months, or when they traveled, the Yokuts constructed small, conical houses and covered them with bark or tule. A large ridged house with two fireplaces, and a door at each end, was also constructed by the Yaudanchi.

The Gashowu and Chukchansi, the northern hill tribes, also built a cone-shaped house with a ring-shaped opening at the top. These dwellings were usually thatched. The floor was possibly lowered about

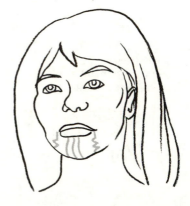

a foot with a digging stick. The diameter of the dwelling was 12 to 15 feet, the height less than that, and the door faced south. It was called a ho, "live", "sit".

There is no reference to thatching tule. The thickness of this rush may have made it more practical for binding or sewing into mats than for bunching into thatch.

The shade, ch'iniu, a flat roof on poles was used by all of the Yokuts. It was a great necessity in the intense heat of the plains in the summer months.

SWEAT HOUSES

The sweat house, mos or mosh, was oblong-shaped, dug down several feet, with a ridge log resting on two posts at the ends, and dirt covered. It was not over 15 feet long and was not used as an assembly chamber or dance house. The older men slept in the sweat house during the winter months, when they were at their home village. The Yokuts had no house for rituals and dances. The rattlesnake, "stepping", the mourning ceremony and other rituals were presented in a large, open, roofless enclosure of brush, resembling a fence.

FOOD

The food resources of California were abundant in their variety. When one failed there were countless others to take its place. The Yokuts, like all California Indians, were an omnivorous group. They ate dogs, but these were taboo to all other northern California Indians. Coyote flesh was avoided and the grizzly bear meat was viewed askance, possibly because of religious reasons. The digger pine nuts were eaten raw and whole. They were also treated like small seeds, winnowed in a scoop-shaped basket, pounded into flour and cooked. There is no reference to the Yokuts having acorn granaries.

COOKING TOOLS

Small, shallow cook pots of soft stone (steatite),reddish in color, were used. The pots were dug out with quartz. Angleworms and grubs were possibly stewed in these pots, or fried in their own fat at the edge of the fire. The Yokuts did not use a paddle for stirring the boiling acorn mush, but a stick looped on itself: though it may have been less efficient for stirring,it served well for removing the hot cooking stones.

MORTARS

Their mortar was a pit in granite that was worked until it became too deep to be useful. The women often left their pestles by the permanent mortars. The pestles were somewhat irregular, with little taper and were slightly oval. One or two sides were flat or concave. On the alluvial plains wooden mortars were used out of necessity. Among the Tachi the most used mortar was one of white oak. It was a flat-bottomed wooden block about a foot high and just half of this in diameter. Except for a narrow rim, the upper surface was burned out by fire, but the pounding was done in a smaller doubly sunk hole in the middle. The pestle was the same as used on the bedrock. The wooden mortar was also used by the Choinimni and Chukchansi, the hill Yokuts.

HUNTING TOOLS

Bows for small game were not much more than a shaped stick, but the good bows were smoothed out of mountain cedar wood and sinew-backed. The bow used primarily for hunting was nearly as long as the hunter was tall, and approximately two fingers in width and the thickness of one. The ends were recurved through a curling back of the thick sinew. The ones used for fighting were shorter, flatter, broader and pinched in the middle. The hunting arrow had a long, sharp foreshaft, but had no real head. The deer arrow had a socket foreshaft made without tie or glue so the main shaft disengaged after hitting. It had a flint head. The war arrow measured from the finger tip to the possible pull of the bow. It had a long, notched wooden point and no foreshaft.

BASKETS

Yokuts' baskets were characterized by one individual type: a coiled jar, like a vessel with a flat shoulder constricted though often with a reflaring neck. The pattern was either hexagons, alternate trapezoids or diamonds in red and black, usually in one or more bands. The shoulder was decorated with a horizontal protruding fringe of quail crests. The two-color pattern was lacking among other California tribes, with the exception of the Chumash.

POTTERY

The Yokuts practiced pottery making. It was pressed out of a lump of clay, or shaped by a rough fitting together of clay pieces. Sticky substances, blood or glue, were possibly used for the binding, but the clay was tempered but minimally or casually. There was virtually no decoration, no slip (a clay coating of creamy consistency) and the color was dark to light gray. The shapes varied from globular to cylindrical.

HAIR STYLES

The women wore their hair long, but the men's hair length was variable. When working or hunting, the men and women gathered their hair under a band. When in mourning the men burned their hair off at the neck, and for a close family member the women did the same.

FACE DECORATIONS

Only the women pierced their nose septum for wearing bone ornaments. Tattooing was practiced more among the northern Yokuts than among the southern, and more so by the women. The designs ran in zig-zag lines and rows of dots down the chin, across from the corners of the mouth. Charcoal dust was rubbed into cuts made with obsidian or flint.

WARFARE

There is little known of the Yokuts' warfare. The tribelets possibly acted as a unit when faced with conflict. This may have given them some advantage of solidarity and numbers over their neighbors, but they were evidently a peaceful tribe, and there are no records to show that they were feared. Conflicts between Yokut tribelets were as frequent as with aliens; but with the majority of their neighbors they seem to have been on very friendly terms. There are also no records of the Yokuts having a victory dance or scalp celebration. Some claim that they did not scalp, but this statement may be incorrect.

CHILDBIRTH

When a woman was ready to give birth she sat on the ground

grasping a stake driven in the ground before her. At the time of delivery she was raised by another woman who grabbed her from behind. The umbilical cord was tied with one of the mother's hairs and was cut with a knife of cane or elder wood, according to the area. The Chukchansi buried the cord; the Tachi preserved it with the child wearing it over its abdomen.

SHAMAN

The shaman was referred to as angtu or antu, with a reference by the southern tribes to poisoning: teish,"maker", by the Chukchansi; tuponot by the Tachi. The word teish reappears in the south as tash and teshich gonom with the Tachi, the weather shamans. The Yokuts' shaman owned a spirit. It may have been an animal that changed into a man, or a monster. It might have been dreamed of, met in actuality, or both. It was a substance possessing an independent life and was related to the medicine man, not an injurious object, but an amulet that he swallowed and kept inside his body. Unlike the Salinans, the shaman's power among the Yokuts was unsought. It was obtained from animals or monsters living in the water or,for example,from the visions that appeared in dreams. The rattlesnake shaman had the sun as his spirit, and the bear doctor a bear as his. The rain doctor's powers were more directly associated with a protecting charm than any other spirits.

SPIRITS

All things or beings or supernatural powers were called "chipni" or "tipni", by all of the Yokuts tribes. The Tachi word, "tuponot", is possibly obtained by one of the vowel changing characteristics of the language. Tipni is probably related with tipin, "above", pertaining to sky, high, top, up. It is equal to the words wakanda, orenda, mana, and manitou. Some usages of the term refer to spirits or monsters. In other connections it is likely to be a shaman, a tipni, or that he possess tipni.

MYTHS OF CREATION

The creators were believed to be all animals, with Eagle as their head as a wise and dignified chief. Coyote, his assistant, was often considered ridiculous and ofttimes inefficient, but on some occasions, when not competing with Eagle, he was thought to possess strange powers. He rarely brought disaster into the world; although Meadowlark died as a result of his folly, or the desire of the insect Kokwiteit; but Coyote assisted. He aided in obtaining fire by stealing the sun for tomorrows' world. He advised Eagle to send Duck to dive for earth from the primeval stump which projected from the universe's first water.

A favorite symbol was "limik", the swift, swooping Falcon. He made no sound, was considered·very wise, a brave warrior and he ate nothing but tobacco. He was always a victim in gambling and his supernatural powers were skillful. The Falcon's ecclesiastical assistant was his friend, Raven. The Owl was a very powerful shaman. The Hummingbird was believed to be Coyote's son who surpassed his mythical father. The Antelope was a swift runner, winning from the Deer and helped to steal fire. The Condor was a cannibal, a schemer and a thief, but was overpowered by the Falcon and Eagle when he threatened the latter's authority.

CONCLUSION

There have been many theories as to where the Indians came from, some believing that they were descendants of the Tartars, Africans, Egyptians, Greeks, Carthaginians, Norse, Irish, Basques, Welsh and Huns, who either traveled to North America deliberately or arrived accidently on a stormy sea.

There was a Bering Strait land bridge connecting Siberia with Alaska not just during the last glacial period of the Pleistocene geological epoch, but also during other stages. Some writers and lecturers find it suitable to accept the theory of the early American Indian walking across the land bridge from Siberia to Alaska, perhaps following game or attempting to escape poor conditions in Asia.

The theory of the first American Indians crossing the Bering Strait land bridge, between 10,000 and 15,000 years ago, is still being expounded, although some believe that the time was long before this period, possibly longer than 30,000 years. Fifty-five miles of water separate the two continents, with the Diomede Islands almost halfway between, as it were, as stepping-stones from the Old World to the New. When the Bering Strait freezes over in the winter months, one can walk from Alaska to Siberia. The Eskimos of both countries visited and traded commodities until in recent years the U.S.S.R. banned it.

Men surely seem to have come to America across the land bridge, as there are evidences of early Asian-type artifacts found in old sites in North America. For example, in Central America pottery from an old site was found which resembles pottery from Japan dating several thousand years B.C. If those pieces were influenced by the Japanese, however, it may be suggested that the influence could as well have arrived by boat.

In 1926, George McJukin, a cowboy, searching for cattle that had strayed near the community of Folsom, New Mexico, accidentally uncovered some giant-size bones and stone points that had been spear tips. It was learned through the scientific investigation made that the bones were of bison, a species that had been extinct for over 10,000 years. Embedded in the bones of the long-horned bison were several of the spear tips. During the investigation it was revealed that man, now known as the Folsom man, had hunted the prehistoric bison from Texas to Canada over 10,000 years ago.

The discovery of the Folsom man soon led to the findings of the Llano culture. These people used a spear point with distinguishing characteristics and the Llano points, along with other artifacts connected with that culture have been discovered from Mexico to Alaska, and in each of the connecting states. The Llano man resided in North America at least 2,000 years before the Folsom man.

In a cave in the Sandia mountain range near Albuquerque, New Mexico, archaeologists in 1936 found evidence of man of an even earlier period. He is known as the Sandia man and from bones and ancient campfire sites excavated it is known that he hunted horses at least 25,000 years before the Spanish reintroduced the animal to New Mexico.

The American Indian stalked the gigantic prehistoric animals, and had the weapons for slaying them ten thousand years before Christ. He probably resided, for example, on the shores of a one-time lake in the Mohave Desert of California; he lived in a cave in southern Illinois and hunted caribou in the state now known as New York, and hunted in the woods of Alabama.

Six thousand years ago, three thousand years before the bow and arrow were introduced to North America, the Indians were cultivating corn in the central section of Mexico.

Strong evidence that the Indian has resided in the Americas for many thousands of years and that numerous tribes lived a very civilized life, their civilization equalling that of the ancient civilizations of the European and Asian continents of the same period, cannot be contradicted.

APPENDIX

SALINAN VOCABULARY

acorn mush or soup	Na'sil
acorns	K^c - ap^c
animal's heart	a'u
antlers	etala-k
awl	Teta'xk
basketry hats	Ts! waketE'
beads, pink	Kni el i
brain	exoxo'
brother	ito'l
bunch grass	K! o'i
burden baskets	p E ta 'tL
cloud	pa'—i
cocoon rattle	Tc! oxo'K
coiled baskets	T Eca'
coiled trays	sāma'k^c
corpse	ca'M te L
dog	xute
elder brother	ka'i
enemy	epeselet
eye	cuke'net
father	ek'
feathers, whiskers	ecax
fern	K! e —ciapowat
finger, toe	a—pela'i
fire	ta'a'u'
games	kusku'i
girls	see'l
granaries	K! ata
grandmother	sit-jar
head	a'ak
heart	e—xiwai
hill	t'uLne
hill oak	P^{c}a' pix

holes, caves	te—le'k'
house, my	Tama or Ta' ma
hummingbird	chuparosa
large burden basket	p Eta 'tl
lightning	sokanto
live oak	cxau' Wat
male, man	lu—wa'
moon	tats'o'opi
morning star	macala'k
mortars	Toro'l
mountain	tpoi, tpo—l, tso'la
mouth	e'lek
my house	Tama or Ta' ma
neck	etea—i
night	sm$_a$ 'K'ai
nose	e'net
oak, hill	p^{c}a'pix
oak, live	cxau'WAT
oak, post	p^c ā ^{c}t
oak, white	t' io' i
parent	ienxe'
path, trail	lu'a, lue
pestles	pa 'nE
pink beads	Kni eli
post oak	p^c a^{c}t
quail	ho'mlik
rainbow	saiy—N
rattlesnake	Tet! aut' onE'
seed beater	Tona'L
seed granaries	sap'k'a'
shallow coiled trays	Sama'k^c
shell of egg	ca'lo
shoulder	ita'l
skin, hide	axwe'm

sky	le'ma
small trinket baskets	TopE's
smoke	ta'te,t
son, child	as
spring of water	telukutea'
storm	ta'pit
sun	Na'
testicles	cu—la't, so—lo
thunder	t'e'lowa
to eat or food	Lam
tongue	epa'l
trays	cla
trinket baskets	topE's
tule	K! a' mtE
white oak	t' w' i
white willow	P E sXe' T^c
wind	ts'a—kai
woman	lets'e'
world	emk'we'L

THE ESSELEN VOCABULARY

Numerals

1	pek
2	xulax
3	xulep
4	xamaxus
5	pemaxala
6	pek — walanai
7	xulax — walanai

The occurrence of case suffixes—analogous to those in other California Indian languages—distinguishes the Esselen from the Salinan. Typical examples are "nu" and "manu": nu is instrumental, and manu comitative.

hit me stone-with	pexuisma ciefe-nu
I go thee with	ninenu name-manu
come me with	iyo ene-manu

acorn soup	tse—win
arm, hand	pū
aunt	wa
back	muut
basket	tsila
bear	xūs
birds	tcaphis
bone	se'
bow-arrow	payunax-pagunax, pawi-lotos
boy	ehi—pana—sis
brother-in-law; sister-in-law	to
cheek	po'
child	tci' tci—pana
coyote	matckas
crow	ā
dark, devil	tumas
daughter	ta—pana
day	as — atsa
deer	amisax
dog	qo hutcmas — canaco
eagle	slo
ear	toū
elder brother	pe
elk	cīw
eye	tuX
father	qo'
fire	anix
fish	caKcile
flea	woxewawi — s—tēp
foot	te'm
girl	ta—pana-si
grandchild	ma
grasshopper	tōg
heart	masianex
hunt	xunio

kill	siniwe
knife	kumel
leg	Ū'L
light (luz)	xetsa
liver	āL
man	ehi—nutc
maternal uncle	ta
meat	tosi
moon	tomanis — aci
mother	tug
mother-in-law (father)	mus
mouth	katusnex
my aunt	k—a—wa
my daughter	sole—ta, ni̥(c)—cole—ta
my elder brother	ma—k—pe̥pe
my father	ma—qo̥'qo
my father-in-law	k—mus
my grandchild	ma—k—a—ma
my maternal grandparent	k—nene
my maternal uncle	k—ta—ta
my mother	ma—k—tug
my nephew	k—lcüix
my paternal grandparent	ma—k—a—māma
my paternal uncle	k—ā̇ nüc
my sister-in-law	ma—k—to
my son	ma—k—itc—tu'n
my younger brother	ma—k—its—is
neck	nii
night	itsu
nose	noX
owl	ceew
paternal uncle	nuc
penis	Xot
rabbit	q'u'n
rattlesnake	tselselkamati
skin	paX

smoke	tcaxa
snake	p'co'c
son	pana — xuex
son or daughter	tu'n
stone	ciefe
sun	asi, aci
tooth	sa'
woman	ta—note
younger brother or sister	is

OUR FATHER

Za til i,   mo   quixco   nea pea limaatnil.
Our father who   art   in   Heaven

An zucueteyem na   etsmatz: antsiejtsitia   na
Hallowed   the thy name   come   the

ejtmilina   an   citaha   natsmalog   zui
Thy Kingdom be   done   thy will   on

lac   quicha   nea pea   lima Maitiltac
earth   as   in   Heaven Give us

taha   zizalamaget   zizucanatel ziczia.
today   our food   our daily

Za Manimtilac   na zanayl   quicha na
Forgive us   the debts,   as   the

Kae apanintilica   no zananal. Zi quetza
We   forgive them   the   our debt.

Commanatatilnac   za   aliminta zo na
Let not   us   fall   into the

zuixnia za no jom zig zumtaylitec.
temptation us from evil   defend.

Amen

(Salinan version of the Lord's Prayer)

TRADE ITEMS

Items traded between the Salinans, the Costanoans, the Chumash and the Yokuts:

SALINANS

Supplied to the Yokuts: Shell beads, whole beads. Received from the Mainland Chumash: Steatite vessels, *Columbella* beads, possibly also steatite and wooden vessels.

COSTANOANS

Supplied to the "Tulare Yokuts": Mussels, abalone shells, salt, dried abalone. Received from the "Tulare Yokuts": Piñon nuts.

ISLAND CHUMASH

Supplied to the Mainland Chumash: Chipped stone implements, fish-bone beads, baskets, a dark stone for digging, stick weights. Received from Mainland Chumash: Seeds, acorns, bows, and arrows.

MAINLAND CHUMASH

Supplied to "southern valley Yokuts": Shell beads, whole pismo clam shells, abalone shells, *Olivella* shells, limpet shells, cowry shells, sea urchin shells, dried starfish. To Yokuts: [subgroup not specified] Clam shells, asphaltum, buckskins, obsidian, abalone.

NORTHERN VALLEY YOKUTS

Received from Costanoans: Mussels, abalone, shells.

SOUTHERN VALLEY YOKUTS

Supplied to Mainland Chumash: Fish, obsidian, salt from salt-grass, seed foods, steatite beads, various herbs, vegetables. Received from Mainland Chumash: Shell beads, whole pismo clams and shells, keyhole limpet shells, abalone shells, *Olivella* shells, sea urchin shells, dried starfish, cowry shells. Supplied to Salinan: Whole shells.

BIBLIOGRAPHY
(In order of page reference)

Powell, J. W., "Indian Linguistic Families of America—North of Mexico," *Seventh Annual Report,* Bureau of American Ethnology, Washington: Government Printing Office, 1891. See p. 15 of present volume.

Henshaw, H. W., "A New Linguistic Family in California," *American Anthropology,* vol. III, 1890, pp. 45-49. See p. 15 of present volume.

Taylor, S., "Indianology of California," *California Farmer and Journal of Useful Sciences,* vols. XIII-XX, February 22, 1860, to October 30, 1863, San Francisco; ref. April 5th and 20th, 1860. See p. 15 of present volume.

Kroeber, A. L., "Salinan Family," *Handbook of American Indians,* Bureau of American Ethnology, Bulletin 30, reprinted by California Book Company, Ltd., Berkeley, California, 1953, pp. 11 and 415. See p. 15 of present volume.

Mason, J. Alden, *The Ethnology of the Salinan Indians,* Berkeley: University of California Press, 1912. See pp. 15, 18 and 27 of present volume.

Sparkman, Philip Stedman, *Cultures of the Luiseño Indians,* Berkeley: University of California Press, 1908, p. 209. See p. 26 of the present volume.

Wheeler, George W., *U.S. Geographical Surveys of the Territory of the United States West of the 100th Meridian, Reports,* vol. VII, *Archaeology,* Washington: Government Printing Office, 1879, p. 262. See p. 26 of the present volume.

Culin, Stewart, "Games of North American Indians," *Twenty Fourth Annual Report to the Secretary of the Smithsonian Institution— 1902-1903,* Bureau of American Ethnology, Washington: Superintendent of Documents, 1907, p. 144. See p. 43 of the present volume.

Kroeber, A. L., *Mission Record 19,* Berkeley: University of California Press, 1908. See p. 47 of the present volume.

Fages, Captain Pedro, "Spanish Catalan Volunteers," records of the Mission San Antonio de Padua, 1769. See p. 48 of the present volume.

Palou, Father Francisco, "Life of Junipero Serra," records of the Mission San Antonio de Padua, early 1700's. See p. 48 of the present volume.

Smith, Frances Rand, *The Mission of San Antonio de Padua,* Stanford University Press, 1932.

BIBLIOGRAPHY
(In alphabetical order)

Alden, Roland H., and Ifft, John D., *Early Naturalists in the Far West*, San Francisco: California Academy of Sciences, 1943.

Bancroft, Hubert Howe, *California Pastoral*, San Francisco: The History Company Publishers, 1888.

Bancroft, Hubert Howe, *History of California*, Berkeley: University of California Press, 1904, vols. I-VII.

Bandini, Helen Elliott, *History of California*, New York: American Book Co., 1908.

Culin, Stewart, "Games of North American Indians," *Twenty Fourth Annual Report*, Bureau of American Ethnology, Washington: Government Printing Office, 1907, pp. 3, 809.

Durham, David L., "Geology of the Tierra Redonda Mountains and Bradley Quadrangles, Monterey and San Luis Obispo Counties, California," *Geological Survey Bulletin 1255*, Department of the Interior, Washington: U.S. Government Printing Office, 1969.

Fages, Captain Pedro, "Spanish Catalan Volunteers," records of the Mission San Antonio de Padua, 1769.

Hamlin, Homer, *Water Resources of the Salinas Valley*, Washington: Government Printing Office, 1904.

Heizer, Robert F., *Language Territories and Names of California Tribes*, Berkeley: University of California Press, 1966.

Heizer, Robert F., and Whipple, M. A., *The California Indians*, Berkeley: University of California Press, 1967.

Henshaw, H. W., "A New Linguistic Family in California," *American Anthropology*, vol. III, 1890.

Kroeber, A. L., *Handbook of the Indians of California*, Berkeley: California Book Company, Ltd., 1953.

Kroeber, A. L., *Languages of the Coast of California South of San Francisco*, Berkeley: University of California Press, 1904.

Locke, Raymond Friday, *The American Indians*, Los Angeles: Mankind Publishing Company, 1970.

Mason, J. Alden, *The Ethnology of the Salinan Indians*, Berkeley: University of California Press, 1912.

Merriam, C. Hart, *Studies of California Indians*, Berkeley: University of California Press, 1962.

Palou, Father Francisco, "Life of Junipero Serra," records of the Mission of San Antonio de Padua, early 1700's.

Powell, J. W., "Indian Linguistic Families of America—North of Mexico," *Seventh Annual Report*, Bureau of American Ethnology, Washington: Government Printing Office, 1891, pp. 1-142.

Rambo, Ralph, "Lo, The Poor Indian," *Pioneer Series No. 2 of the Santa Clara Valley*, San Jose, CA: Rosicrucian Press, 1967.

Smith, Frances Rand, *The Mission of San Antonio de Padua*, Stanford University Press, 1932.

Sparkman, Philip Stedman, *Culture of the Luiseño Indians*, Berkeley: University of California Press, 1908.

Starr, Frederick, *American Indians*, Boston: D.C. Heath and Company, 1898.

Taylor, S., "Indianology of California," *California Farmer and Journal of Useful Sciences*, San Francisco, 1860 et seq.

Wheeler, George W., *U.S. Geographical Surveys of the Territory of the United States West of the 100th Meridian, Reports*, vol. VII, *Archaeology*, Washington: Government Printing Office, 1879.

INDEX

pomo indians of california and their neighbors

The Pomos were not actually a tribe in the true sense, but a group of tribelets speaking similar languages and dialects. As with most California Indians, their culture has been little understood by white people and often wrongly looked upon because of lack of understanding.

The smashing of the Pomos' culture by conquest was very complete, but the old Indian spirit is beginning to return, and we need to encourage their pride and self-respect as well as a return of the beautiful elements of their culture that make them distinctive.

Volume one of the American Indian Map Book series, this book attempts, and succeeds, in bridging a long-standing cultural gap between the Pomo Indians and other tribes and races, and brings understanding for these unique people.

Pomo Indians of California and Their Neighbors is a must for those seeking America's Indian heritage. It can be purchased at your nearest bookstore, or by writing Naturegraph Books.